Beckton's Railways and Locomotives

Dave Marden

Kestrel Railway Books
PO Box 269
SOUTHAMPTON
SO30 4XR

www.kestrelrailwaybooks.co.uk

Printed by the Amadeus Press

ISBN 978-1-905505-38-8

Front cover:
Dwarfed by its industrial surroundings, Neilson No 5228 takes on water at Beckton Gas Works on 30th April 1960. Within a few more weeks this loco had been broken up. (R C Riley/Transport Treasury)

Back cover:
Two rare colour views of Beckton's locomotives taken by Philip Kelly in 1955.
Top: *Peckett No 1837 of 1931 as Gas Works No 37 pictured near the Roundhouse loco shed sporting the company's apple green livery.*
Bottom: *Another Beckton Peckett. This time at the Products Works where No 1576 of 1921 is seen in the local maroon livery running as No 11.*

Contents

Those who have lived in the era of a gas works will remember them as devilish grim and grimy places, covered in a film of coal dust and emitting pungent odours, but to enthusiasts of industrial railways they were sheer heaven. Many such works had their own private lines for transporting coal for the process of extracting gas from it, and some had both standard and narrow gauge systems. In general, gas works ceased production in the mid to late 1960s when natural gas from the North Sea began to be pumped ashore and distributed around the national networks.

There can be few railway enthusiasts that have not heard of Beckton Gas Works as it was the biggest in Europe, with a huge internal railway operated by numerous and distinctive cut-down locomotives, running throughout both the Gas Works and the adjacent Products Factory. Beckton's railways lasted for a century, during which time around a hundred locomotives came and went, working ceaselessly around the clock to provide heat and energy for London.

Also included are details of the neighbouring Outfall and Sewage Works, which had its own railway and also saw a host of contractor's engines engaged there over the years. *Beckton's Railways and Locomotives* gives an insight to this fascinating corner of London's industrial past.

Dedication

To the Martins of Hoxton
My long lost family

Introduction and Acknowledgements

When compiling my two books on London's Dock Railways, it soon became apparent that the Port of London was not the only large industrial railway system on the Thames. Although the docks railways were huge, there were many other large concerns along the banks of the river that also had considerable lines of their own. Gasworks, power stations, engineering works and manufacturing plants were among an almost continuous belt of industries that grew along its course.

In the main, these industries were constructed east of the city, down river from the docks, on what was barren marshland at the time. One such development was the huge Beckton Gas Works, together with its Products Works, which made for a massive concentration of industrial railways in a relatively small area.

There can be few railway enthusiasts that have not heard of Beckton Gas Works and its immense railway network, but now, like so many heavy industries, it is consigned to history as just a distant memory more than four decades after its closure. The Beckton locos with their exposed footplates and cut down appearance were universally regarded as something special. With the change from steam to diesel much of the magic disappeared before the Beckton system closed, but it is hoped this book will go some way towards keeping its memory alive.

To complete the Beckton story, the adjacent Sewage Works with its narrow gauge railway has also been included but, like its big neighbour, it is now almost forgotten.

The following people and publications have proved important sources of information:

- Industrial Railway Society – Various publications and articles
- Industrial Locomotive Society – Various publications and articles
- *Gas Light & Steam* by Malcolm Millichip
- *Disused Stations Website* by Nick Catford
- *British History Online Website*
- *Chemicals from Coal (GLIAS)* by Cyril Arthur Townsend
- Peter Smith – former Regional Director of British Gas, North Thames

The abbreviations for locomotive manufacturers are as follows:

AB: Andrew Barclay, Sons & Co Ltd, Kilmarnock
AE: Avonside Engine Co Ltd, Bristol
AW: Sir W G Armstrong, Whitworth & Co (Engineers) Ltd, Newcastle-upon-Tyne
B: Barclay & Co, Kilmarnock
Beckton: Gas Light & Coke Co, Beckton Gas Works
BgC: Baguley Cars Ltd, Burton-on-Trent, Staffs
BgDC: Baguley Cars Ltd, Burton-on-Trent, Staffs / Agents Drewry Car Company Ltd, London
BH: Black, Hawthorn & Co Ltd, Gateshead
CF: Chapman & Furneaux Ltd, Gateshead
Chaplin: Alexander Chaplin & Co Ltd. Crantonhill Works, Glasgow
DK: Dick, Kerr & Co Ltd, Britannia Engineering Works, Kilmarnock
FH: F C Hibberd & Co Ltd, Park Royal, London
GE: George England & Co Ltd, Hatcham Ironworks, London
HC: Hudswell, Clarke & Co Ltd, Railway Foundry, Leeds
HE: Hunslet Engine Co Ltd, Hunslet, Leeds
MR: Motor Rail Ltd, Simplex Works, Bedford
MW: Manning, Wardle & Co Ltd, Boyne Engine Works, Leeds
N: Neilson & Co Ltd. Springburn Works, Glasgow
NR: Neilson Reid & Co, Glasgow
P: Peckett & Son Ltd, Atlas Engine Works, Bristol
RH: Ruston & Hornsby Ltd, Lincoln
RSH: Robert Stephenson & Hawthorns Ltd, Newcastle-upon-Tyne
S: Sentinel (Shrewsbury) Ltd, Battlefield Works, Shrewsbury
WB: W G Bagnall Ltd, Castle Engine Works, Stafford
WSO: Wellman Smith Owen Engineering Corporation Ltd, Darlaston, Staffs

CHAPTER 1

Beckton Gas Works

The Gas Light & Coke Company 1870-1902

The Gas Light & Coke Company (GLCC) was formed in 1812 and built many works for producing coal gas in and around London, the largest and most famous of which being that at Beckton. Its main works for supplying the capital had been at Westminster but, as the city grew, it became increasingly difficult to keep up the production of gas according to demand.

One of the major difficulties was the supply of coal, which was delivered by barges, these being hampered by tides and general congestion on the Thames. The GLCC therefore decided to build a larger works down river at Gallions Reach to the west of Barking Creek where coal could more easily be transported to the water frontage by colliers. Gas would then be transported by way of a 48 inch main to the Westminster works for distribution around the city's network.

Until the later construction of the Royal Albert Docks, the area had been bleak marshland with few local inhabitants and, such was the impact of the gas works on the district, it took the name of Beckton, after Simon Adams Beck, Governor of the company.

The company purchased around 600 acres of land and construction commenced in 1868 under the direction of engineers F J Evans, J Orwell Phillips and V Wyatt, with the main contractor being John Aird. It was one of London's largest engineering projects and the first gas was produced from 25th November 1870. Even so, construction continued to expand the works until 1882.

Construction under way at Beckton c1869 with steam power driving the cutting edge machinery. The long single-length ladder may have caused problems in transit. (Author's Collection)

The huge Beckton Gas Works was the biggest in Europe and possibly the world. In London, its railway became the second largest private system after that of the docks, having 42 miles of track, nine of which were at an elevated level. Coal arrived from the north east of England in colliers and was discharged at two river piers.

The first pier (No 1) was built in 1870, where tracks led directly to the overhead railway that encircled the works on steel viaducts 22 feet above the ground. It ran between, and into, the retort houses which were arranged in six parallel pairs that eventually grew to fourteen in total. At various places along its route were open spaces between the rails where coal could be deposited by hopper wagons down to stockpiles on the ground below.

The rails at ground level served most buildings around the works and were mainly for the transportation of coke and general freight, with the two levels being connected by three inclines. The coal stockpiled on the ground was loaded into trains by rail-mounted grab cranes, then transported up the inclines by a loco with up to six loaded wagons, pushing them up a 1 in 30 gradient after a speedy run at around 20mph.

Handling of coal shipments subsequently switched to the second Pier (No 2), which was completed in 1893 where twelve hydraulic cranes, fitted with grabs, could each lift a ton of coal per minute. After this, No 1 pier was used for discharging coke to barges until it was rebuilt in 1926 and the two piers exchanged duties.

Gas was extracted by heating coal in the retort houses, the process leaving residues of coke and various liquors and oils. The gas then had impurities removed before passing through exhauster houses that pumped it into the mains network. While the coke was sold off as fuel, the Beckton Works also set up an adjacent factory for the manufacture of by-products from its gas production, such as tar, creosote and ammonia. This began operation in 1879 and within a couple of years had developed its own internal railway, which was connected to the Gas Works but operated entirely independently from it, although locos from each system would often cross paths during their duties (see the Products Works Chapters 6 and 7).

Above: *Engineers and dignitaries gather for a historic photo marking the dawn of Beckton Gas Works. (Author's Collection)*

Right: *Inside one of the retort houses at Beckton Gas Works around the turn of the century, where a rail mounted hydraulic stoker feeds coal to the insatiable furnaces. (Author's Collection)*

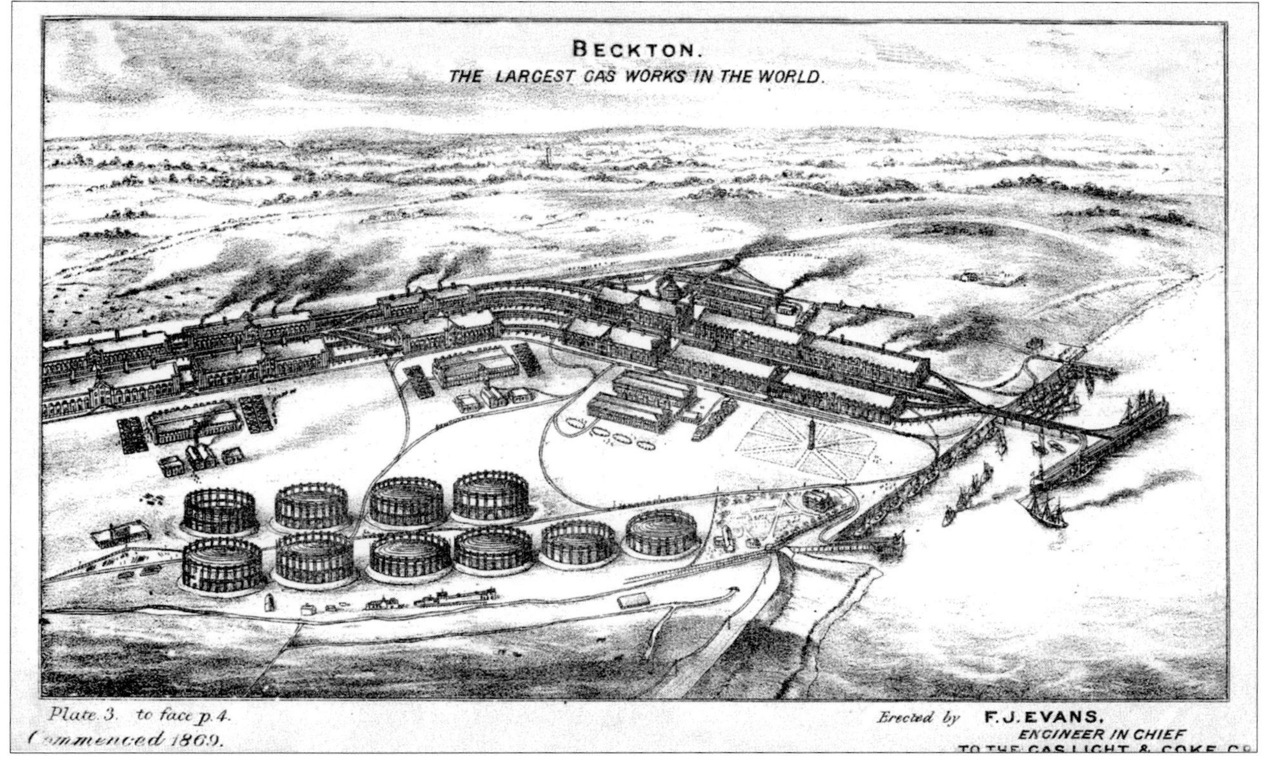

A drawing of Beckton Gas Works in its early stages shows how rural the surrounding area was in those days. (Industrial Locomotive Society Collection)

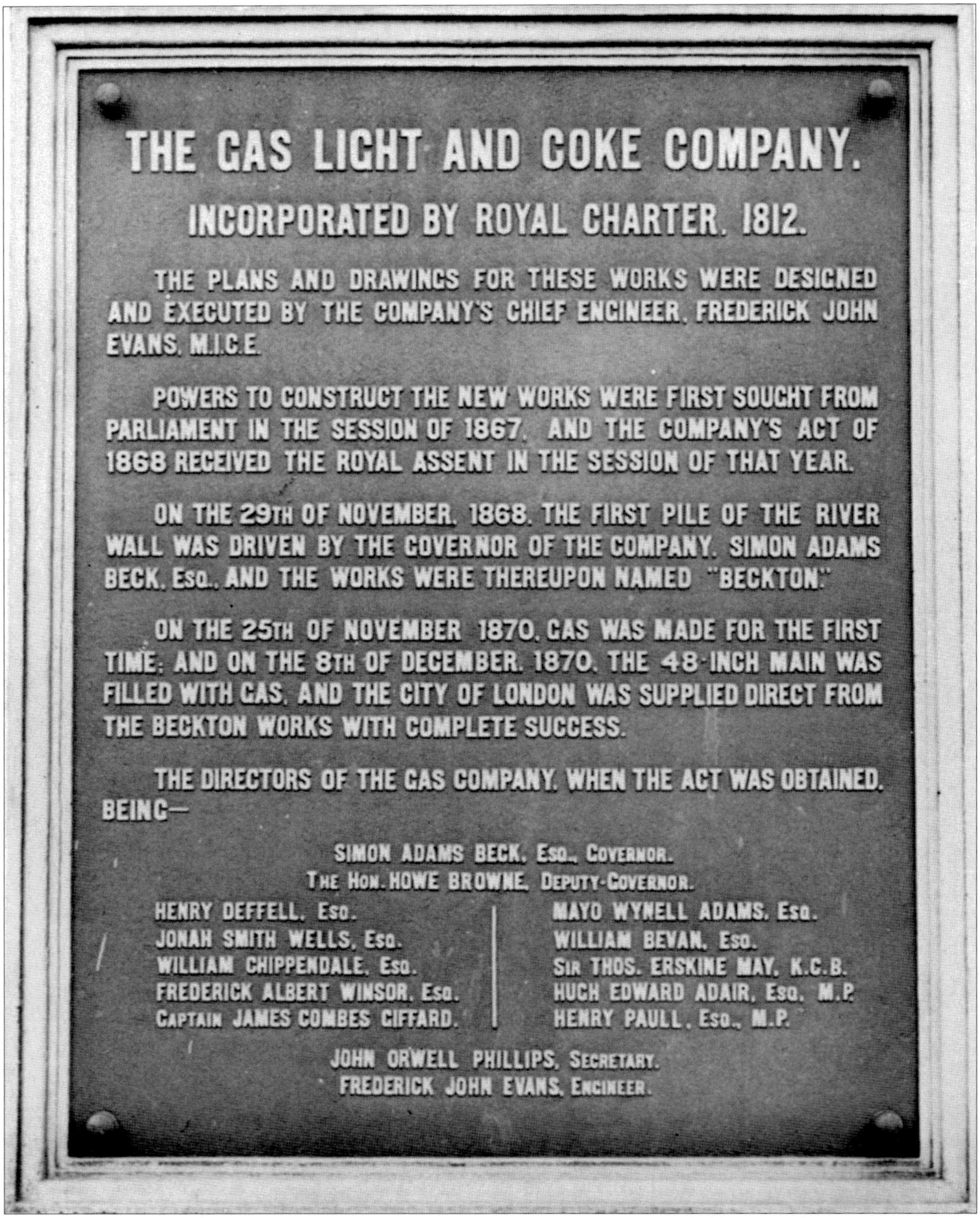

THE GAS LIGHT AND COKE COMPANY.

INCORPORATED BY ROYAL CHARTER. 1812.

THE PLANS AND DRAWINGS FOR THESE WORKS WERE DESIGNED AND EXECUTED BY THE COMPANY'S CHIEF ENGINEER, FREDERICK JOHN EVANS, M.I.C.E.

POWERS TO CONSTRUCT THE NEW WORKS WERE FIRST SOUGHT FROM PARLIAMENT IN THE SESSION OF 1867, AND THE COMPANY'S ACT OF 1868 RECEIVED THE ROYAL ASSENT IN THE SESSION OF THAT YEAR.

ON THE 29TH OF NOVEMBER, 1868, THE FIRST PILE OF THE RIVER WALL WAS DRIVEN BY THE GOVERNOR OF THE COMPANY, SIMON ADAMS BECK, ESQ., AND THE WORKS WERE THEREUPON NAMED "BECKTON."

ON THE 25TH OF NOVEMBER 1870, GAS WAS MADE FOR THE FIRST TIME; AND ON THE 8TH OF DECEMBER, 1870, THE 48-INCH MAIN WAS FILLED WITH GAS, AND THE CITY OF LONDON WAS SUPPLIED DIRECT FROM THE BECKTON WORKS WITH COMPLETE SUCCESS.

THE DIRECTORS OF THE GAS COMPANY, WHEN THE ACT WAS OBTAINED, BEING—

SIMON ADAMS BECK, ESQ., GOVERNOR.
THE HON. HOWE BROWNE, DEPUTY-GOVERNOR.

HENRY DEFFELL, ESQ.
JONAH SMITH WELLS, ESQ.
WILLIAM CHIPPENDALE, ESQ.
FREDERICK ALBERT WINSOR, ESQ.
CAPTAIN JAMES COMBES GIFFARD.

MAYO WYNELL ADAMS, ESQ.
WILLIAM BEVAN, ESQ.
SIR THOS. ERSKINE MAY, K.C.B.
HUGH EDWARD ADAIR, ESQ., M.P.
HENRY PAULL, ESQ., M.P.

JOHN ORWELL PHILLIPS, SECRETARY.
FREDERICK JOHN EVANS, ENGINEER.

A tablet erected on the wall of No 5 Exhauster House marking the GLCC's historical achievements at Beckton. (Author's Collection)

Looking southwards over the elevated railway in Beckton's early years with the cranes of No 2 Pier visible on the far left as, to the right, a lone Neilson loco rumbles over a stockpile of coal on the ground below. (John Alsop Collection)

A view from 1899 shows Beckton's two piers with a collier at No 1. The barges carried coke to the city and coal to other gas works along the Thames. (Author's Collection)

To connect its remote location to the metropolis, the GLCC built a branch line that joined the North Woolwich Railway near Custom House and ran to a new station at its Beckton works (see Chapter 5). In its early days the company employed around 2000 workers, the bulk of them being transported in from Canning Town and East and West Ham, but some of the workforce were housed in 120 homes built along Winsor Terrace (named after the founder of the GLCC, Frederick Albert Winsor). These were to the west of the new station and housed key workers such as engineers, foremen and railway men who would need to be on call. One such family was that of the Dobbs who lived at No 88 and of whom at least two generations were employed at the GLCC. John Dobbs, was an engine driver at Beckton for almost 40 years and his son, Bertram James Dobbs, was an apprentice at the workshops.

For the inhabitants of this small estate, facilities included a chapel, school, post office, shops, a pub and a cricket ground for recreation. At its height, the works covered around 400 acres and employed over 6000 men, being the largest gas works in Europe. It also operated 17 colliers, which discharged 1000 tons of coal each day at the Thames piers.

The huge internal railway operated under a sophisticated signalling system of semaphores and colour lights, these being orange and blue rather than the traditional red and green so as not to conflict with the nearby shipping navigation lights. The whole complex was controlled by 14 signal boxes, three of which were on the upper level and, despite its complexities, few, if any, accidents or derailments were reported during its history. The importance of the railway at Beckton cannot be overstated as the constant and increasing demand for energy to the capital meant that it was employed 24 hours a day with a huge dependence on its locomotives. These were, until the latter years, maintained in pristine condition with immaculate paintwork, being the pride of both the company and the men who drove them, and with the Works Engineer personally testing them on arrival or after overhaul.

The first locomotive on the Beckton site was that

Beckton's No 1 Pier and the Gas Works elevated railway are shown in another illustration from 1899. (Author's Collection)

of chief contractor John Aird & Sons. This was a nearly new Manning Wardle saddle tank No 221 named *Kingston* that arrived in 1869 and remained until the works were completed in the following year.

The three original locos employed by the gas company were well tank engines supplied new by makers Neilson and Co of Glasgow in 1870. As with all the types that followed them, these were four coupled engines, a limitation dictated by the sharp curves of the works railway. Nos 1561 and 1562 were originally named *Alderman* and *R A Gray* respectively, running as Nos 1 and 2. The pair had open footplates devoid of a cab structure – as did most of those that followed. When operating on the upper level and out on the piers during inclement weather, conditions for loco crews must have been atrocious but the men steadfastly refused the protection of enclosed cabs and it wasn't until the much later arrivals that such shelter materialised.

The third Neilson loco arrived new in 1872, this was No 1659 named *Hon. Howe Browne,* and all three worked on the upper level, hauling coal from the North (No 1) Pier to the retort houses.

Standard couplings on Beckton locos consisted of a three link chain with a hook on the end, and one of the features of Beckton locos were ropes from the footplate to the hooks, the one to the front buffer beam running along the boiler and over the smokebox. This enabled wagons to be uncoupled by the firemen who

Station and District Intelligence

BECKTON NOTES.

J. DOBBS.

Mr. J. Dobbs, a locomotive driver at Beckton for nearly forty years, has now retired on the pension granted to him by the Directors. An interesting meeting took place in the Loco. lobby at Beckton, on Thursday, July 10th, when Mr. Dobbs was presented with a marble clock, subscribed for by his fellow workers. Mr. Wood, Superintendent Mechanical Engineer, presided, supported by Mr. Mills; and both gentlemen spoke very highly of our co-partner and old chum Dobbs. It has also been decided to present a hand-bag to Mrs. Dobbs. We wish them both long life and happiness.

J. D.

Above: *No 88 Winsor Terrace was the home of the Dobbs family, of whom two generations worked at Beckton Gas Works. This view from the garden looking south towards the railway sidings was taken in the 1920s. (T M Sanderson Collection)*

Left: *A cutting from the Co-Partners Magazine, which carried an article marking the retirement of driver John Dobbs in 1913 after almost 40 years service at Beckton. (T M Sanderson Collection)*

A photo from the late 1800s shows one of the early Neilson locos with a train on one of the piers. Judging by its tall chimney, the engine was not one that ventured into the restricted entrances of the retort houses. Just discernible are men wearing top hats in the centre of the picture and a man atop the rigging of the ship alongside. (Peter Smith Collection)

were known as "rope runners". Several of the locomotives were fitted with air pumps for supplying a continuous compressed air pipe connected to the doors of hopper wagons. These were discharged by the rope runner who operated a valve on each wagon. Also common to all Beckton locos (apart from the latter day diesels) was their large wooden dumb buffers to avoid locking on the tight curves around the works railway.

The coke handling and ash disposal at ground level was operated by horses until the appearance of a trio of engines built by Alexander Chaplin & Co of Glasgow (Nos 1675, 1756 and 1757). All were purchased new in 1874, the first being ordered in January that year and the other pair in June. Chaplin locos had vertical boilers, their appearance being a sharp contrast to standard tank engines, and these were of a special design to accommodate the low entrances to the retort houses. The Chaplins were allocated running numbers 1, 2 and 3, so it would seem there was a duplicate ground level numbering system, being quite separate from that of the Neilsons running above. Their time at Beckton seems not to have gone beyond the turn of the century as reports of the loco stock around the early 1900s make no reference to them.

The Chaplins were augmented by a Manning Wardle saddle tank, No 457 that carried the name of company governor *Simon Adams Beck,* and was delivered new in 1875. This became No 4, after which the number series became consecutive with both high and low level engines in the same sequence. In an early report there is a suggestion that No 457 worked passenger trains between Beckton and Custom House but this would be most improbable as the branch was operated by the GER before its arrival. More likely, it might have hauled passenger stock from Beckton station and into the works itself (see Chapter 5).

A standard item of equipment for locos working on the ground level was a coke fork. The various heaps of coal and coke stockpiled around the site often subsided on to the tracks and had to be cleared for trains to pass.

Neilson No 1561 as originally built is shown in this works photo with the name "Alderman" above its makers plate. The flimsy canopy over the cab was dispensed with during its time at Beckton. (Industrial Locomotive Society Collection)

This photo of Neilson No 5087 (No 25), taken c.1900 from a public footpath that once crossed the works but was closed at the outbreak of WWI, has two main points of interest. Firstly, the driver is in uniform and secondly, the coke fork carried on the front buffer beam. This was used to clear occasional slips of coal and coke that obstructed the track. (Industrial Locomotive Society Collection)

Beckton Gas Works Contract - Aird 0-4-0ST Manning Wardle No 221

Name:	*Kingston*
Manufacturer:	Manning Wardle & Co Ltd
Built:	1866
Works number:	221
Cylinders:	9in x 14in
Driving Wheels:	2ft 9in
Wheelbase:	4ft 9in
Water Tank Capacity:	250gals
Boiler pressure:	120psi
Weight	10ton 17 cwt
At Beckton Gas Works:	1869 – 1870

Contractors John Aird & Sons were engaged to construct the Gas Works at Beckton in 1868 and one of their many locos worked on the contract from 1869. Named *"Kingston"* Manning Wardle No 221 was supplied to Aird on 30th November 1866. No 221 had previously worked on Aird's contract for the Tooting to Wimbledon line before finding itself at Beckton in 1869. After the works were completed in 1870 it was later employed in various other Aird works, including Tilbury Docks between 1884 and 1886 where it carried the running No 100, before transfer to fellow contractors Flower & Everett at the Rainham Rubbish Shoot around 1905 where it spent its final days before disposal.

Manning Wardle locomotive No 221 "Kingston" and crew pictured when working for John Aird & Sons. (Peter Smith Collection)

GLCC Beckton Gas Works 0-4-0WT Neilson No 1561

Name:	*Alderman (Lord Mayor)*
Manufacturer:	Neilson & Co Ltd
Built:	1870
Works number:	1561
Running number:	No 1
Length:	17ft 4in
Height:	8ft 2in
At Beckton Gas Works:	1870 – 1963

No 1561 arrived new in 1870, being the first of many from this maker to run the rails at Beckton Gas Works, operating on the high level railway while hauling coal from Pier No 1. It was originally supplied with a rudimentary cab canopy but this was dispensed with. In its early days it carried the name *Alderman* but Neilson's records show this to be *Lord Mayor.* Having been rebuilt at the gas company's own workshops in 1929 it continued to give sterling service over an incredible 93 years. In its latter years No 1561 was maintained in pristine condition and afforded only light duties until its retirement in 1963. It was then taken into preservation at Penrhyn Castle Museum, north Wales in December that year and remains there today.

GLCC Beckton Gas Works 0-4-0WT Neilson No 1562

Name:	*R A Gray*
Manufacturer:	Neilson & Co Ltd
Built:	1870
Works number:	1562 (rebuilt as S 6951)
Running number:	No 2
At Beckton Gas Works:	1870 – 1927 (and 1927 – 1938 as S 6951)

Neilson No 1562 arrived in 1870 with No 1561, both being 0-4-0 well tank engines. In 1927 the gas company decided to experiment. The Sentinel Company rebuilt this engine as a vertical boilered geared tank using the original chassis and parts of their own design. The work was carried out between May and October 1927 and Beckton No 2 emerged in its new form (see notes for Sentinel No 6951 in Chapter 2).

GLCC Beckton Gas Works 0-4-0WT Neilson No 1659

Name:	*Hon. Howe Browne*
Manufacturer:	Neilson & Co Ltd
Built:	1872
Works number:	1659
Running number:	No 3
At Beckton Gas Works:	1872 – 1934

The third Neilson loco arrived in 1872 bearing the name *Hon. Howe Browne*, after the then Deputy Governor of the company the Hon. Richard Howe Browne and was, in most respects, similar to the two earlier arrivals from that maker. After some 62 years of service it was withdrawn from service and scrapped in 1934 along with several others considered past redemption.

Beckton's first Neilson loco No 1561 pictured on the turntable inside the Gas Works Roundhouse on 9th June 1934. On the left is its sister engine, formerly No 1562 but now converted to Sentinel No 6951. Note the gas lighting around the shed. (H F Wheeller Collection)

Beckton's third Neilson well tank was No 1659 and originally carried the name "Hon. Howe Browne", which had long disappeared before this photo was taken in the 1930s. (Peter Smith Collection)

GLCC Beckton Gas Works 0-4-0VBT Chaplin No 1675

Manufacturer:	Alexander Chaplin & Co Ltd
Built:	1874
Works number:	1675
Running number:	No 1
Cylinders:	5.75in x 11in
Boiler pressure:	100psi
At Beckton Gas Works:	1874 – c. 1900

Other than their identities, little is known about the trio of Chaplin locos that worked coke trains from the Beckton retort houses. They were all supplied new in 1874 and No 1675 was ordered in January and dispatched to Beckton on 27th May that year. At least one of them was still evident when the photograph opposite was taken around the turn of the century. It is thought they might have been disposed of around that time.

GLCC Beckton Gas Works 0-4-0VBT Chaplin No 1756

Manufacturer:	Alexander Chaplin & Co Ltd
Built:	1874
Works number:	1756
Running number:	No 2
Cylinders:	5.75in x 11in
Boiler pressure:	100psi
At Beckton Gas Works:	1874 – c. 1900

First of a pair of Chaplin locos ordered by the Gas Light & Coke Company for Beckton in June 1874. No 1756 was supplied on 29th September that year, with sister No 1757 following on 15th October. As with the other Chaplins, their time at Beckton lacks information and they were probably disposed of around the turn of the century

GLCC Beckton Gas Works 0-4-0VBT Chaplin No 1757

Manufacturer:	Alexander Chaplin & Co Ltd
Built:	1874
Works number:	1757
Running number:	No 3
Cylinders:	5.75in x 11in
Boiler pressure:	100psi
At Beckton Gas Works:	1874 – c. 1900

The second of two Chaplin locomotives supplied new in 1874. No 1757 was ordered in June that year and arrived on 15th October, bringing the Chaplin contingent at Beckton to three. Like the others, this one was probably scrapped and replaced around 1900.

Left: *One of the three Chaplin locos engaged in hauling coke wagons at Beckton is pictured there with its crew in the early 1900s. (John Hutchings Collection/Industrial Railway Society)*

Below: *Another photo showing one of the Beckton Chaplin locos at the Gas Works, possibly around the turn 20th century, with an internal coal wagon also pictured. (Peter Smith Collection)*

GLCC Beckton Gas Works 0-4-0ST Manning Wardle No 457

Name:	*Simon Adams Beck*
Manufacturer:	Manning Wardle & Co Ltd
Built:	1875
Works number:	457
Running number:	No 4
Cylinders:	10in x 17in
Driving Wheels:	3ft 1in
Wheelbase:	5ft 0in
Boiler pressure:	120psi
Weight:	16ton 0 cwt
At Beckton Gas Works:	1875 – 1931

As a departure to the previous Neilson locos, the Gas Company ordered a saddle tank engine from Manning Wardle & Co of Leeds. This was a standard class F engine but was designed with a height restriction of 8ft 3in in accordance with the confines of the gas works. It was dispatched from the maker's works to Beckton on 5th April 1875 and carried the name *Simon Adams Beck* after the Governor of the Gas Company, from whom the district of Beckton took its name. Unlike the previous Neilsons that worked on the high level railway, Beckton No 4 was employed below on the ground system. Its time at Beckton lasted until it was broken up around 1931.

In a departure from their early purchases from Neilson & Co, Beckton turned to Manning Wardle for their fourth locomotive. This was No 457 which, at one time, carried the name of the Company Governor, "Simon Adams Beck". The driver with the moustache is John Dobbs who served in that capacity for almost 40 years and lived in retirement at Winsor Terrace. He was the great grandfather of the owner of this photograph. (T M Sanderson Collection)

To avoid confusion, references to the following locos will not include further running numbers as these were changed and duplicated over the years as engines were scrapped, replaced, rebuilt and renumbered. To add to this perplexity, the locomotive fleet at the associated Products Works was numbered in the same series. Many of the locos listed below arrived as replacements for their predecessors and full details of their comings and goings can be found in the individual locomotive profiles. Although a few locos latterly served in both the gas works and the by-products factory, their details appear only in the location where they began operation.

The majority of Neilson engines supplied to Beckton were of similar design and the following dimensions apply to the locomotives unless specified otherwise:

Cylinders:	10in x 18in
Driving Wheels:	2ft 10in
Wheelbase:	5ft 0in
Boiler Pressure:	120psi
Weight:	16ton 0cwt

As production at the works increased, four more locos from Neilson arrived between 1876 and 1878. Nos 2151 *(Queen's Counsel),* 2227, 2228 and 2380 were all well tanks like their predecessors, but the following batch of five more Neilsons were side tank engines. These were Nos 2382, 2465, 2466, 2597 and 2598, arriving new between 1878 and 1880.

GLCC Beckton Gas Works 0-4-0WT Neilson No 2151

Name:	*Queen's Counsel*
Manufacturer:	Neilson & Co Ltd
Built:	1876
Works number:	2151
Running number	No 5
At Beckton Gas Works:	1876 – 1927

Following the one-off purchase of Manning Wardle No 457 in the previous year, Beckton returned to Neilson for their next loco. *Queen's Counsel* arrived new in 1876 and was the last named engine at Beckton. Its time there lasted until it was scrapped in 1927.

No 2228 was one of the early Neilson well tank locos and is pictured in Beckton Gas Works Long Shed in 1934, just prior to disposal. (See page 17.) (C L Turner/Industrial Locomotive Society)

GLCC Beckton Gas Works 0-4-0WT Neilson No 2227

Manufacturer: Neilson & Co Ltd

Built: 1877

Works number: 2227

Running number No 6

At Beckton Gas Works: 1877 – 1934

One of two Neilson locomotives purchased in 1877, the other being No 2228. The pair operated for the same period until deemed worn out in 1934 when they, and several others, were scrapped.

No 2227 as Gas Works No 6 was one of the original Neilson well tank engines supplied in the 1870s. (Peter Smith Collection)

GLCC Beckton Gas Works 0-4-0WT Neilson No 2228

Manufacturer: Neilson & Co Ltd

Built: 1877

Works number: 2228

Running number: No 7

At Beckton Gas Works: 1877-1934

The second of two Neilson locomotives delivered new in 1877, the other being No 2227. After 57 years of service the pair was considered beyond repair and both met their end in 1934.

GLCC Beckton Gas Works 0-4-0WT Neilson No 2380

Manufacturer: Neilson & Co Ltd

Built: 1878

Works number: 2380

Running number: No 8

At Beckton Gas Works: 1878 – 1934

No 2380 was the last well tank loco supplied to Beckton by makers Neilson & Co, but by no means the final engine from that company as many more followed, the rest being side tank designs. Having arrived in 1878 it worked until 1934 when, along with several others, it was broken up and replaced.

GLCC Beckton Gas Works 0-4-0T Neilson No 2382

Manufacturer: Neilson & Co Ltd

Built: 1878

Works number: 2382

Running number: No 9

Driving Wheels: 3ft 1in

At Beckton Gas Works: 1878 – 1938

Neilson No 2382 was the first 0-4-0 tank loco supplied to Beckton. Arriving new in 1878 it had slightly larger wheels than its predecessors from that maker, and served at the gas works until scrapped in 1938.

GLCC Beckton Gas Works 0-4-0T Neilson No 2465

Manufacturer: Neilson & Co Ltd

Built: 1879

Works number: 2465

Running number: No 10

Driving Wheels: 18ft 2in

Height: 8ft 1in

At Beckton Gas Works: 1879 – 1962

Arriving new in 1879, Neilson No 2465 was of the standard dimensions from that maker but was altered in 1929 when it was rebuilt at Beckton's workshops. It re-emerged with 2ft 9in wheels and a working order weight of 15ton 10cwt. This was the second such re-build carried out by the company and its working life was prolonged until 1962 when it was finally consigned to the scrap heap.

Neilson No 2380 was the last well tank design supplied to Beckton. It is seen here running as No 8 on 9th July 1927. (H C Casserley)

Beckton's loco No 9 was first of their Neilson side tank locos. No 2382 is shown in ex-works condition with a painted number, before receiving its metal plate version at the Gas Works. (Glasgow University/Peter Smith Collection)

Neilson No 2465 as Beckton No 10 pictured on 21st February 1953. (L R Freeman /Transport Treasury)

GLCC Beckton Gas Works 0-4-0T Neilson No 2466

Manufacturer:	Neilson & Co Ltd
Built:	1879
Works number:	2466
Running number:	No 11
Length:	18ft 2in
Height:	8ft 1in
At Beckton Gas Works:	1879 – 1961

This loco was the second of a pair to arrive new from Neilson's in 1879. Its initial dimensions being the same as its sister until it became the first loco to be rebuilt at Beckton under a programme that began in 1928. It returned from the workshops with 2ft 9in wheels but its working weight had been increased to 17ton 1cwt. Like No 2465 its working life was considerably extended, lasting until scrapped in 1961.

GLCC Beckton Gas Works 0-4-0T Neilson No 2597

Manufacturer:	Neilson & Co Ltd
Built:	1880
Works number:	2597
Running number:	No 12
Cylinders:	12in x 20in
Driving Wheels:	3ft 1in
Weight:	20ton 0cwt
Length:	19ft 8in
Height:	8ft 6in
At Beckton Gas Works:	1880 – 1960

1880 saw a slightly different design from Neilson's. No 2597 arrived new that year but differed from earlier types by having larger cylinders, wheels, longer side tanks and being somewhat heavier overall. It was rebuilt at Beckton in 1931 with smaller wheels of 3ft 0in and its weight slightly reduced to 19ton 7cwt. Its service at Beckton ended when it was cut up on site by George Cohen Sons & Co in May 1960.

GLCC Beckton Gas Works 0-4-0T Neilson No 2598

Manufacturer:	Neilson & Co Ltd
Built:	1880
Works number:	2598
Running number:	No 13
Length:	18ft 2in
Height:	8ft 1in
At Beckton Gas Works:	1880 – 1967

The second of two 1880 arrivals was No 2598. This was of the standard Neilson dimensions supplied to Beckton and was rebuilt at the Gas Company workshops in 1929, prolonging its working life until scrapped in February 1967, being one of the last surviving locos there.

Neilson No 2466 is seen in a line of locos outside the Roundhouse Shed on 18th June 1955. Also in the picture are locos No 39 (AB No 1722) with No 38 (Hudswell Clarke No 522) nearest the shed. (Philip J Kelley)

Beckton's No 12 was one of many Neilson products to earn its keep at the gas works, being slightly larger than its predecessors No 2597. It remained there for 80 years. (Douglas Clayton Collection/Industrial Railway Society)

One of two 1880 arrivals at Beckton was Neilson No 2598, seen here running as No 13. (Douglas Clayton Collection/ Industrial Locomotive Society)

The next three Neilsons purchased were altogether different, being odd looking saddle tanks, of a cut down design, enabling them to work in the height restricted areas. Nos 3097, 3345, and 3451 were supplied new between 1883 and 1885 and became known as "Jumbos" due to their elephant like appearance.

For some reason, the next two purchases in 1886 were from another maker, Black, Hawthorn & Co of Gateshead. The first was No 865, a saddle tank similar to the Neilsons, but No 864 was a conventional tank loco, both though were cabless, like those before them.

After their brief dalliance with Black Hawthorn, the company returned to Neilson for their next batch of purchases. Between 1888 and 1897 eleven new locos were supplied by them. These were Nos 3789, 4249, 4250, 4414, 4408, 5086, 5087, 5228, 5229, 5230 and 5231. Nos 4408 and 5086 were both departures from the previous designs in that they had enclosed cabs for the protection of crews when working lime trains of open wagons.

Left: *A rare sight at Beckton. This photo taken c. 1900 shows Neilson No 4408 (No 23) with its cab in place, which afforded a degree of safety to crews working with lime trains. (Industrial Locomotive Society Collection)*

Below: *The first Neilson saddle tank loco at Beckton was No 3097, which ran as Gas Works No 14. (Peter Smith Collection)*

GLCC Beckton Gas Works 0-4-0ST Neilson No 3097

Manufacturer:	Neilson & Co Ltd
Built:	1883
Works number:	3097
Running number:	No 14
At Beckton Gas Works:	1883 – 1935

Neilson No 3097 arrived as Beckton No 14 in 1883 as the first of the "Jumbo" saddle tanks and seems to have led a fairly hum-drum life before being scrapped in 1935.

GLCC Beckton Gas Works 0-4-0ST Neilson No 3345

Manufacturer:	Neilson & Co Ltd
Built:	1884
Works number:	3345
Running number:	No 15
At Beckton Gas Works:	1883 – 1930

The second Neilson "Jumbo" saddle tank, No 3345, supplied to Beckton, arrived new in 1884 and was given the running number 15. Like its sister No 3097 it seems to have had an uneventful life before being broken up in 1930.

GLCC Beckton Gas Works 0-4-0ST Neilson No 3451

Manufacturer:	Neilson & Co Ltd
Built:	1885
Works number:	3451
Running number:	No 16
Length:	19ft 0in
Height:	6ft 7in
At Beckton Gas Works:	1885 – 1958

The third Neilson saddle tank, No 3451 was supplied new in 1885, arriving as Beckton No 16. Having been rebuilt in the gas company workshops in 1936, its wheels were reduced to 2ft 9in with a lesser working weight of 15ton 4cwt. It remained in service until scrapped by George Cohen Sons & Co in August 1958.

Neilson No 3451 was one of the early "Jumbo" saddle tanks, pictured here as Beckton No 16. (Douglas Clayton Collection/Industrial Railway Society)

GLCC Beckton Gas Works 0-4-0ST Black, Hawthorn No 865

Manufacturer:	Black, Hawthorn & Co Ltd
Built:	1886
Works number:	865
Running number:	No 17
Cylinders:	10in x 18in
Driving Wheels:	2ft 10in
Wheelbase:	5ft 0in
Boiler pressure:	120psi
Weight:	16ton 0cwt
At Beckton Gas Works:	1886 – 1958

In a departure from their usual supplier, Neilsons, the gas company purchased two locomotives in 1886 from the Gateshead firm of Black, Hawthorn & Co. The first of these was No 865, which left the makers works on 29th March. Having been rebuilt at the Beckton workshops in 1936 it lasted until 1958 when it was scrapped by George Cohen, Sons & Co in August that year.

GLCC Beckton Gas Works 0-4-0T Black, Hawthorn No 864

Manufacturer:	Black, Hawthorn & Co Ltd
Built:	1886
Works number:	864
Running number:	No 18
Cylinders:	10in x 18in
Driving Wheels:	2ft 10in
Wheelbase:	5ft 0in
Boiler pressure:	120psi
Weight:	16ton 0cwt
Length:	19ft 0in
Height:	6ft 7in
At Beckton Gas Works:	1886 – 1959

One of two Black Hawthorn locos dispatched to Beckton on the same day, 29th September 1886. Although their works numbers were consecutive, they were very different in appearance: No 864 being a tank engine and No 865 having a saddle tank. Unlike its sister it was not rebuilt at the GLCC workshops but was sent away for repair after suffering damage during a WWII air aid in January 1941. It afterwards worked on until 1959 when it was scrapped on site by the firm of Drew & Sawyer from Belvedere, Kent.

GLCC Beckton Gas Works 0-4-0T Neilson No 3789

Manufacturer:	Neilson & Co Ltd
Built:	1888
Works number:	3789
Running number:	No 19
Cylinders:	12in x 20in
Driving Wheels:	3ft 1in
Weight:	20ton 0cwt
Length:	19ft 8in
Height:	8ft 6in
At Beckton Gas Works:	1888 – 1962

Neilson No 3789 was sent new to Beckton in 1888 as No 19 in the gas works fleet. At 20 tons it was a little heavier then the standard design from this maker, having extended side tanks. It was rebuilt at the Beckton workshops in 1931 and its term of service lasted until it was scrapped in 1962.

Beckton's No 17 (BH 865 of 1886) stands idle in the round-house shed at the gas works. (Douglas Clayton Collection/ Industrial Railway Society)

The gas works second Black, Hawthorn loco was No 864 but it differed from No 865, being an engine with side tanks in-stead of a saddle. (Douglas Clayton Collection/Industrial Railway Society)

No 3789 was one of heavier Neilson engines with extended tanks, it is seen here as No 19 inside the Beckton Roundhouse on 9th July 1927. (H C Cas-serley)

GLCC Beckton Gas Works 0-4-0T Neilson No 4249

Manufacturer:	Neilson & Co Ltd
Built:	1890
Works number:	4249
Running number:	No 20
Length:	18ft 2in
Height:	8ft 1in
At Beckton Gas Works:	1890 – 1960

Beckton's No 20 was one of a pair of Neilsons delivered new in 1890 and was of the maker's standard design adopted by the gas works at that time. No 4249, arrived with No 4250 (a saddle tank loco) and, having been rebuilt at Beckton in 1929, it lasted one more year than its sister, being scrapped on site by George Cohen, Sons & Co in May 1960.

GLCC Beckton Gas Works 0-4-0ST Neilson No 4250

Manufacturer:	Neilson & Co Ltd
Built:	1890
Works number:	4250
Running number:	No 21
Length:	19ft 0in
Height:	6ft 7in
At Beckton Gas Works:	1890 – 1959

One of a pair of Neilson engines delivered to Beckton Gas Works in 1890. The two locos were different in that sister No 4249 was a tank loco but No 4250 was a saddletank. Having been rebuilt at Beckton in 1938 it survived until being broken up on site in June 1959 by the firm of Drew & Sawyer from Belvedere, Kent

GLCC Beckton Gas Works 0-4-0T Neilson No 4414

Manufacturer:	Neilson & Co Ltd
Built:	1891
Works number:	4414
Running number:	No 22
Cylinders:	12in x 20in
Driving Wheels:	3ft 1in
Wheelbase:	5ft 0in
Boiler pressure:	120psi
Weight:	20ton 0cwt
Length:	19ft 8in
Height:	8ft 6in
At Beckton Gas Works:	1891 – 1960

Neilson No 4414 was one of the Beckton locos that had extended side tanks to the front of the smokebox, therefore its working weight was higher than many of the gas works locos. It was rebuilt at Beckton in 1931 and worked on until being scrapped on site by the Southend firm of H F A Dolman in November 1960.

A lone cyclist pedals past a silent Neilson No 4249 nearing the end of its time at Beckton. (Peter Smith Collection)

A second 1890 arrival at Beckton was Neilson No 4250 which became No 21 in the gas works order. (Jack Faithfull/RCTS)

The cut down design of Beckton locos enabled them to overcome the restricting height of the retort house entrances. Neilson No 4414 demonstrates the confines on 22nd April 1959. (Sydney A Leleux)

GLCC Beckton Gas Works 0-4-0T Neilson No 4408

Manufacturer:	Neilson & Co Ltd
Built:	1892
Works number:	4408
Running number:	No 23
Length:	18ft 2in
Height:	8ft 1in
At Beckton Gas Works:	1892 – 1967

Neilson No 4408 ran as gas works No 23, having arrived at Beckton in 1892. Unusually, this loco was fitted with a cab in its earlier days, but that had been removed by 1934. Having been rebuilt at the company workshops in 1929 it lasted until scrapped in 1967.

GLCC Beckton Gas Works 0-4-0T Neilson No 5086

Manufacturer:	Neilson & Co Ltd
Built:	1896
Works number:	5086
Running number:	No 24
Length:	18ft 2in
Height:	8ft 1in
At Beckton Gas Works:	1896 – 1958

The first of two 1896 arrivals from Neilson, No 5086 was another loco that, at one time, had a cab, which had been subsequently removed by 1934. In the meantime, it had been rebuilt at Beckton in 1930 and remained in service until August 1958 when it was scrapped by George Cohen, Sons & Co.

GLCC Beckton Gas Works 0-4-0ST Neilson No 5087

Manufacturer:	Neilson & Co Ltd
Built:	1896
Works number:	5087
Running number:	No 25
Length:	16ft 0in
Height:	6ft 7in
At Beckton Gas Works:	1896 –1961

The second of two arrivals at Beckton in 1896, No 5087 was rebuilt at the gas company's workshops in 1938. Its time at Beckton ended in May 1961 when it was transferred to Southall Gas Works. By the 25th October that year, it had been taken into preservation by the Industrial Locomotive Society and stored at Sheffield Park on the Bluebell Railway in Sussex. August 1967 saw another move, this time to the Bressingham Steam Museum at Diss, Norfolk where it remains today.

Gas Works No 23 was Neilson No 4408 of 1892 vintage. It was rebuilt at Beckton in 1929 and is seen there on 9th June 1934. (H F Wheeller Collection)

Beckton's No 24 was Neilson No 5086 and was photographed on 30th October 1954. (H D Bowtell/Industrial Locomotive Society)

Neilson No 5087 was one of Beckton's "Jumbos" and was photographed outside the roundhouse shed on 24th August 1957. (R C Riley/Transport Treasury)

GLCC Beckton Gas Works 0-4-0T Neilson No 5228

Manufacturer:	Neilson & Co Ltd
Built:	1897
Works number:	5228
Running number:	No 26
Length:	18ft 2in
Height:	8ft 1in
At Beckton Gas Works:	1897 – 1960

One of four more Neilson locos to arrive in 1897, No 5228 was one of the earlier engines to be rebuilt at Beckton in 1929, prolonging its working life until May 1960 when it was cut up on site by George Cohen, Sons & Co.

GLCC Beckton Gas Works 0-4-0T Neilson No 5229

Manufacturer:	Neilson & Co Ltd
Built:	1897
Works number:	5229
Running number:	No 27
Length:	18ft 2in
Height:	8ft 1in
At Beckton Gas Works:	1897 – 1962

The second of four new Neilson locos to arrive in 1897, No 5229 seems to be one of the few engines that were not rebuilt at the gas company's workshops. However, its working life prevailed until it was scrapped in 1962.

GLCC Beckton Gas Works 0-4-0T Neilson No 5230

Manufacturer:	Neilson & Co Ltd
Built:	1897
Works number:	5230
Running number:	No 28
Length:	18ft 2in
Height:	8ft 1in
At Beckton Gas Works:	1897 – 1962

The third of four Neilson locos to arrive new in 1897, No 5230 was rebuilt at Beckton in 1930 and remained in service until being broken up in 1962.

GLCC Beckton Gas Works 0-4-0T Neilson No 5231

Manufacturer:	Neilson & Co Ltd
Built:	1897
Works number:	5231
Running number:	No 29
Length:	18ft 2in
Height:	8ft 1in
At Beckton Gas Works:	1897 – 1962

The last of a quartet of locos built by Neilson to arrive at Beckton in 1897. No 5231 was rebuilt at the local workshops in 1930 and remained in service at the gas works until transferred to the Products Works on 15th June 1962. There it remained for a further five years before being scrapped in July 1967. (See page 32 for an illustration of this loco.)

Dwarfed by its industrial surroundings, Neilson No 5228 takes on water at Beckton Gas Works on 30th April 1960. Within a few more weeks this loco had been broken up. (R C Riley/ Transport Treasury)

Running as Gas Works No 27, Neilson No 5229 was captured on camera underneath one of the elevated railway sections on 26th October 1957. (L R Freeman/Transport Treasury)

Neilson No 5230 at work with coke wagons outside the Long Shed near the maintenance workshops on 9th June 1934. (H F Wheeller Collection)

As previously stated, the company had considerable resources and facilities at its workshops for rebuilding and repairing their rolling stock, but in 1902 it was decided to expand into actual locomotive building. Two engines were produced as Beckton: Nos 1 and 2, with running numbers 30 and 31, to a design that was remarkably similar to the previous engines supplied by Neilson, who, some sources suggest, considered legal action. Although this never resulted, it is worth noting that no more were built at Beckton and no further engines were supplied to the gas works by Neilson, who became partners in the North British Locomotive Company in 1903. Alternatively, could it be that following Neilson's bold new venture, they were unable, or unwilling, to supply Beckton's railway with further locomotives?

After completion of Beckton locos Nos 1 and 2, the Gas Works engines totalled 31 with an internal rolling stock consisting of 1,336 trucks. Of these, 305 were coal wagons, 481 coke wagons with 550 general purpose types including tipper trucks for transporting ash and clinker from the retort houses to the waste tips. The whole operation ran over some 40 miles of track where up to 30 trains were continually in operation at any time.

Left: *The works plate of the second Beckton built locomotive produced at the company's workshops in 1902. The design of the two engines was remarkable similar to that of Neilson. (H C Casserley)*

Below: *Neilson No 5231 passing a piece of "modern" concrete architecture (an overhead pipeline support) on 4th October 1958. (H C Casserley)*

The extensive locomotive workshops at Beckton could handle all manner of repairs and rebuilds, and even produced two of their own engines. (Peter Smith Collection)

GLCC Beckton Gas Works 0-4-0T GLCC No 1

Manufacturer:	Gas Light & Coke Company
Built:	1902
Works number:	1
Running number:	No 30
Weight:	16ton 9cwt
Length:	18ft 2in
Height:	8ft 1in
At Beckton Gas Works:	1902 – 1960

The Gas Light & Coke Company had, for so many years, purchased the majority of locomotives from the firm of Neilson & Co. The Beckton workshops were so ably equipped for heavy repairs to their locomotives, they decided to build their own and two were produced in 1902, running as Nos 30 and 31. However, the design adopted was so remarkably similar to that of Neilson's there were rumours of litigation, though this never came about. The outcome was that no more were built at Beckton and no further engines were supplied to the gas works by Neilson. No 30, as it was numbered, survived until May 1960 when it was scrapped on site by George Cohen, Sons & Co

No 30 was the first of two Beckton self-built locomotives. Their near total replication of the Neilson design was said to cause some concern to the Glasgow company who, afterwards, supplied no more engines to the gas works. (L R Freeman/Transport Treasury)

Another view inside the impressive locomotive workshops at Beckton. (Peter Smith Collection)

GLCC Beckton Gas Works 0-4-0T GLCC No 2

Manufacturer:	Gas Light & Coke Company
Built:	1902
Works number:	2
Running number:	No 31
Weight:	16ton 11cwt
Length:	18ft 2in
Height:	8ft 1in
At Beckton Gas Works:	1902 – 1959

The second, and final, locomotive turned out of Beckton's own workshops also appeared in 1902 as No 31, after which additional engines were obtained from a variety of builders. Beckton No 2 was adopted as "Pride of the fleet" and reserved for prestigious duties such transporting VIPs around the works, the most notable occasion being the visit of their Majesties King George V and Queen Mary, who toured the works and opened the new coal handling plant on 10th July 1926. The loco was kept in pristine condition with a highly polished dome and brasswork until its grandeur was finally ended when it was scrapped on site in June 1959 by the firm of Drew & Sawyer of Belvedere in Kent. Its ceremonial duties were then taken up by a refurbished Neilson No 1561, the original gas works engine No 1.

Beckton's second home produced locomotive ran as No 31, having an illustrious career as pride of the fleet and first choice engine for VIP visits. (Author's Collection)

The Beckton built No 31 with the engineers and apprentices involved in its construction. The young man seated on the tank beside the chimney is Bertram James Dodd, son of the driver featured in the photo of MW No 457. (T M Sanderson Collection)

Beckton's original shed was the Roundhouse, built in 1875. This picture taken on 30th May 1960 shows its distinctive octagonal shape. The loco in the foreground is Barclay No 1720. (R C Riley/Transport Treasury)

Left: *A photo taken in 1934 shows the arched northern entrance of the brick building that adjoined the Roundhouse at its southern end with the corrugated Long Shed built alongside it. The Armstrong Whitworth diesel loco can be seen in the shed. (Industrial Locomotive Society Collection)*

Right: *The sheer size and complexity of the Beckton Gas Works railway is shown in this 1914 map, which does not include that to the Products Works whose connection is shown at the top left. The overhead lines ran from the river piers at bottom right, through the retort houses and encircled the works, while the outfall sewer is shown running left to right across the top. (Crown Copyright)*

CHAPTER 2

Beckton Gas Works

The Gas Light & Coke Company 1902-1949

At its full extent, the gas works railway extended to some 41 miles, with 32 miles of track at ground level, and a further nine on the overhead sections. The works had over 1000 wagons for internal use for transporting coal, coke and general waste.

The company had its own workshops where maintenance of locos and rolling stock was carried out, even to the extent of completely rebuilding engines, and there were two main loco sheds located at the north east of the works.

Initially, the locomotives were accommodated and serviced in the Roundhouse Shed, an octagonal building with a two road northern extension built in 1875. The main building had 15 roads radiating from its 20ft diameter central turntable, eight of which incorporated inspection pits. As the loco fleet grew, an additional structure, known as the Long Shed, was built alongside the extension, incorporating the original building's western wall in its construction. This could house up to 20 engines and, when the earlier building was demolished, the wall was retained as an integral part of the shed. The rest was mainly of corrugated metal and had a high, rounded roof. Following damage by bombing in WWII the roof was replaced by a simple apex design which appears in many photos taken in the 1950s. After the establishment of the Long Shed, the old Roundhouse was principally used for storing locos that were out of use or awaiting repair.

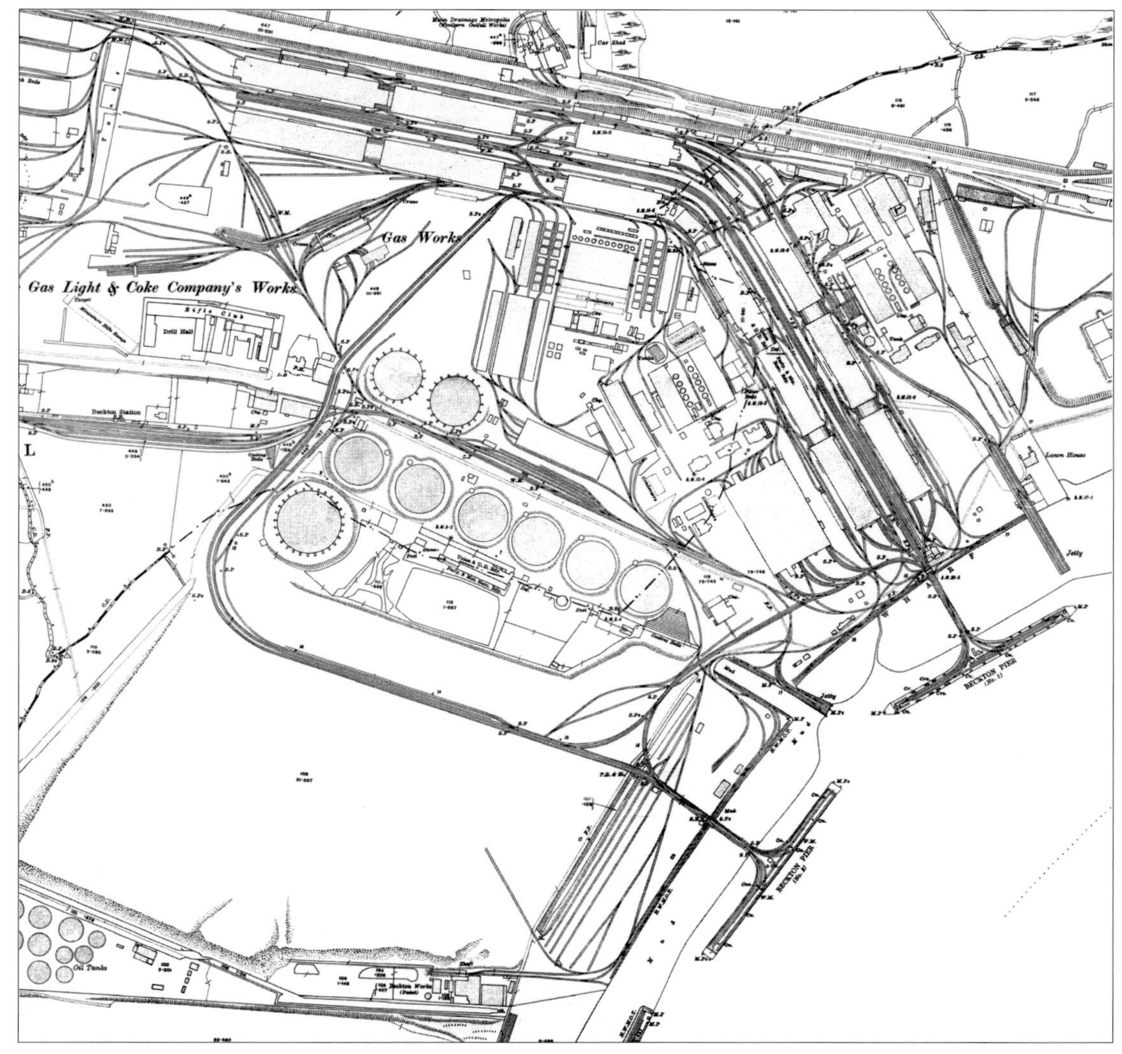

An eerie scene inside the cathedral-like Roundhouse Shed as Neilson locos (L-R) Nos 5230, 4249, 5229 and 4408 stand in silence on 22nd April 1959. The shed was originally gas lit but the later hooks around the walls at window level were for hanging lanterns. (Sydney A Leleux)

The long shed as originally built, showing the rounded roof and partly enclosed northern end. Barclay No 1721 (Beckton No 36) and Neilson No 2597 (No 12) complete the scene on 9th June 1934. (H F Wheeller Collection)

An unusual elevated view of locos in the Long Shed where it can be seen the roof was missing. At the top right is the wall of an earlier building that was retained as part of the structure. The old round-topped design was replaced by a simple apex roof following damage in the Second World War. (Peter Smith Collection)

Also in the days under the old roof, locos in the Long Shed simmer in readiness for their turns of duty. (Peter Smith Collection)

Both Beckton sheds are on view in this photo from 29th August 1957. By then, the Long Shed had been rebuilt with an apex roof. Neilson Nos 1561 (No 1) and 5087 (No 25) stand in the foreground. (H C Casserley)

The pair of locomotives built at Beckton were kept in pristine condition for use on special occasions, such as the Royal visit in 1926. To transport dignitaries around the works, a plush saloon was available and reserved for such duties. At this point is worth noting the standard livery of the gas works engines was green, originally with black bands and yellow lines, later changing to black bands with white lining. The connecting rods and number plates were red. Locos at the Products Works were painted maroon with similar lining but also carried their running numbers on the smokebox doors.

After the Neilson episode in 1902, further locomotive purchases were from other manufacturers and 1909 marked a new departure when Manning Wardle No 901 was acquired second hand from dealers Thomas W Ward at Silvertown. This had previously been a contractor's engine but its time at Beckton lasted only until 1912 when it was transferred to Bromley-by-Bow Gas Works. At the outbreak of World War One another Manning Wardle, No 1832, was bought new from the makers but, throughout the rest of the conflict, new locomotives were in short supply and further arrivals would be second hand. During this period three engines built by Andrew Barclay Sons & Co of Kilmarnock (Nos 636, 262 and 957) arrived from various sources. These were followed after the war by two anonymous saddle tanks (one is thought to be AB No 266) about which little is recorded, along with two more saddle tanks built by Hudswell Clarke (Nos 287 and 657). These two arrived at the end of the war and the two "unknowns" were sent away in 1918 and 1920 respectively.

GLCC Beckton Gas Works 0-4-0ST Manning Wardle No 901

Name:	*(Fanny), (Harboro'), (Rose)*
Manufacturer:	Manning Wardle & Co Ltd
Built:	1885
Works number:	901
Running number:	No 32
Cylinders:	9in x 14in
Driving Wheels:	2ft 9in
Wheelbase:	4ft 9in
Boiler pressure:	120psi
Weight:	10ton 17cwt
Water capacity:	250gals
Length:	15ft 4in
At Beckton Gas Works:	1909 –1912

Manning Wardle No 901 arrived at Beckton after passing through several owners. Having been dispatched by the makers on 19th January 1885 to contractors Kellet & Bentley, bearing the name *Fanny,* it worked on the construction of the LSWR Christchurch to Brockenhurst line before being sold to fellow contractor J T Firbank in 1887 who took over the contract until its completion in 1888. Firbank then took the loco to work on the Acton to Northolt line for the GWR where its name was changed to *Harboro'* . That contract ended in 1905 but the firm ceased trading in 1906 and the loco went to dealers T W Ward at Silvertown. 1909 saw its move to Beckton where it became No 32, working there until transferred to Bromley-by-Bow gas works in 1912. There it received its third name *Rose* which it carried until disposed of for scrap in 1927. (See page 43 for an illustration of this loco.)

GLCC Beckton Gas Works 0-4-0ST Manning Wardle No 1832

Manufacturer:	Manning Wardle & Co Ltd
Built:	1913
Works number:	1832
Running number:	No 32
Cylinders:	10in x 16in
Driving Wheels:	2ft 9in
Wheelbase:	5ft 0in
Boiler pressure:	120psi
Weight:	16ton 17cwt
Length:	18ft 2in
Height:	7ft 10in
At Beckton Gas Works:	1913 – 1955

Manning Wardle No 1832 was dispatched new to Beckton on 17th October 1913, being a replacement for MW No 901 that had been sent to work at Bromley-by-Bow. It also took up its predecessor's running number becoming Beckton's second No 32. Although being one of the maker's F Class engines, it differed greatly from their standard design to meet the requirements of the GLCC. In comparison to other Beckton locos its time there was relatively short and ended when scrapped in June 1955.

GLCC Beckton Gas Works 0-4-0ST Barclay No 636

Manufacturer:	Andrew Barclay Sons & Co Ltd
Built:	1889
Works number:	636
Running number:	No 33
Cylinders:	11in x 18in
Driving Wheels:	3ft 0in
At Beckton Gas Works:	1916 – 1949

This locomotive was originally built as No 295 in 1887 and was eventually dispatched from the maker's works as No 636 on 29th August 1889 when sent new to contractors Morrison & Mason at Paisley. By March 1903 it was engaged in their construction of the Alloway to Girvan line and by 1912 it had found its way to Portsmouth Dockyard where new locks and gates were being built. On completion of the works in 1916 the loco was sold to Beckton, via dealers B Goodman in June that year. Having suffered damage during a World War Two air raid in 1940 it was sent for repair the following year and returned only to last until being scrapped in 1949.

Beckton's second Manning Wardle loco was No 901, a much travelled former contractor's engine. (Peter Smith Collection)

Manning Wardle No 1832 became Beckton's second No 32 when it replaced MW 901 in 1913 and is pictured there on 9th July 1927. (H C Casserley)

Several of contractor Morrison & Mason's former locos found their way to Beckton Gas Works. One was AB No 636, which ran as No 33, and was pictured there on 9th June 1934. (H F Wheeller Collection)

GLCC Beckton Gas Works 0-4-0ST Barclay No 262

Manufacturer:	Andrew Barclay Sons & Co Ltd
Built:	1883
Works number:	262
Running number:	No 34
Cylinders:	11in x 18in
Driving Wheels:	3ft 3in
At Beckton Gas Works:	1916 – 1935

Having been built in 1883, AB No 262 was dispatched from the maker's works on 4th February 1884 to the firm of Steel & Turner at Barrasford, Northumberland, after which it came to Beckton via dealers B Goodman in August 1916 and remained in service until scrapped in 1935.

GLCC Beckton Gas Works 0-4-0ST Barclay No 957

Manufacturer:	Andrew Barclay Sons & Co Ltd
Built:	1902
Works number:	957
Running number:	No 35
Cylinders:	10in x 18in
Driving Wheels:	3ft 0in
At Beckton Gas Works:	1917 – 1949

Another locomotive to arrive at Beckton during WWI was Barclay No 957. This loco had been dispatched on 4th February 1903 to contractors Morrison & Mason for their construction works on the Alloway to Girvan line, where it was employed until 1908 before being transferred to M&M's contract for new locks and gates at Portsmouth Dockyard. At the end of that contract it was sold to dealers B Goodman from where it came to Beckton in March 1917 at a cost of £605.00. Its service ended when scrapped in 1949.

GLCC Beckton Gas Works 0-4-0ST Barclay No 266

Name:	*(Peggy)*
Manufacturer:	Andrew Barclay Sons & Co Ltd
Built:	1884
Works number:	266
Running number:	No 36 (or No 39)
Cylinders:	11in x 18in
Driving Wheels:	3ft 3in
At Beckton Gas Works:	1917 – 1918

Details of two locos at Beckton, Nos 36 and 39 are a little vague. They both came from contractor Morrison & Mason's contract at Portsmouth Dockyard and both were at Beckton in 1918. AB No 266 was delivered new to M&M at Paisley for work on the Port Eglinton Junction at Glasgow until 1885. It was then engaged on the Alloway to Girvan line from 1902 until that contract was completed in 1906. It was afterwards employed on a Portsmouth Dockyard contract from 1908 until around November 1914 after which wartime service saw it taken to the War Department's camp at Catterick, Yorkshire by June 1917. In the same year it came to Beckton via dealers J F Wake but by 1918 it had been transferred to Bromley-by-Bow gas works where it was given the name *Peggy* and scrapped there on an unknown date.

Barclay No 262 as Beckton's No 34 outside the Long Shed at the Gas Works on 9th July 1927. (H C Casserley)

Barclay No 957 at Beckton Gas Works where it was a wartime arrival as No 35 in 1917. (Industrial Locomotive Society Collection)

AB No 266 made a brief appearance at Beckton before being transferred to Bromley-by-Bow gas works where it was pictured in the loco shed. (Industrial Locomotive Society Collection)

GLCC Beckton Gas Works 0-4-0ST Hudswell, Clarke No 657

Name:	*(Lillian)*
Manufacturer:	Hudswell, Clarke & Co Ltd
Built:	1903
Works number:	657
Running number:	No 38
Cylinders:	10in x 16in
Driving Wheels:	2ft 9.5in
At Beckton Gas Works:	1918 – 1938

This loco began life as a contractor's engine and was with the firm of C J Wills when it carried the name *Lillian*. It was sold to the New Explosives Co Ltd at Stowmarket, Suffolk in May 1915, working there through WWI until sold to the GLCC at Beckton in 1918, where it remained until scrapped in 1938.

GLCC Beckton Gas Works 0-4-0ST Barclay Number not known

Manufacturer:	Andrew Barclay Sons & Co Ltd
Running number:	No 39 (or No 36)
At Beckton Gas Works:	1918 – 1920

The second of two mystery locos that came to Beckton around 1917/1918 from Morrison & Mason's contract at Portsmouth Docks, where most of those used were supplied by Andrew Barclay. One of these was AB No 266 (see page 44), but details of the second are not known, other than it was transferred to the Bromley-by-Bow works around October 1920.

GLCC Beckton Gas Works 0-4-0ST Hudswell, Clarke No 287

Name:	*(Maggie)*
Manufacturer:	Hudswell, Clarke & Co Ltd
Built:	1887
Works number:	287
Running number:	No 37
Cylinders:	10in x 16in
Driving Wheels:	2ft 9in
At Beckton Gas Works:	1919 – 1930

This was possibly Beckton's most travelled loco. Having been dispatched new on 12th November 1887 to the firm of W P Hartley in Liverpool, HC No 287 moved to the Electro Chemical Company at St Helens in 1895. It was then sold to contractor Sir John Jackson around 1900 and was used during the construction of Ferrol Dockyard in Spain between 1909-1913. Upon returning home it found itself at the Ministry of Munitions, Gretna during WWI before being purchased by the GLCC at Beckton in 1919 where it worked until scrapped in 1930.

1919 saw the resumption of buying new locomotives when the Hunslet Engine Company supplied No 1335. This was followed in 1920 by a Baguley petrol railcar No 790 which was a converted lorry chassis with flanged wheels for ferrying goods and personnel around the works. Next came three more locos from Andrew Barclay (Nos 1720, 1721 and 1722) all new in 1921 and then another Baguley conversion, No 1335, in 1923. It is not known how long the Baguley vehicles remained in service but they were probably disposed of by the late 1930s.

In 1926, coal handling at No 2 Pier transferred back to a much revamped No1. Here, modern electric cranes loaded coal on to a conveyor that carried the fuel to a new storage bunker installed nearby for coal distribution around the works on the upper level. This could hold up to 6,000 tons and discharge simultaneously into rail wagons via six rows of 16 chutes positioned over six tracks. The 16 chutes were able to fill a 16 wagon train positioned directly beneath them. So efficient was the process that an entire train could be loaded with 80 tons in just one minute. The trains would then move off to fuel the retort houses and return for more in a continuing process on a scale that is difficult to envisage.

Hudswell, Clarke No 657 as gas works No 38 photographed outside the old Long Shed at Beckton on 9th June 1934. The unsuccessful diesel loco, AW No D23, stands idle on the left of the photo. (H F Wheeller)

New cranes and hoppers line Pier No 1 for the discharge of coal from vessels to a new 6,000 ton capacity coal bunker. This facility had been modernised in 1926. (Peter Smith Collection)

Right: *Beckton's first home built loco, running as No 30, hauls a coke train over the level crossing at the Gas Works entrance in the 1930s. Note the pillars supporting the overhead railway towering above the gates. (J W Sparrow Collection)*

Left: *One of the Neilson locos hauls a coal train over the elevated railway from the pier towards the retort houses. This was a never ending process operating 24 hours a day. (Peter Smith Collection)*

The waterfront at Beckton showing the conveyor for transferring coal up from the pier to the 6000 ton capacity storage bunker. The photograph was taken at Beckton on 4th October 1958. (H C Casserley)

Looking westwards along the high level tracks, which seem to stretch forever, there is almost an air of the fairground as Neilson No 4408 guides a party of guests packed aboard an open balconied observation car on 9th August 1927. (H C Casserley)

In 1927 one of the early Neilsons, No 2151, was scrapped while another of the original pair, No 1562, was rebuilt as vertical-boilered, geared tank by the Sentinel Company of Shrewsbury as their No 6951. However, this does not seem to have been a success as the experiment was not repeated. From 1928 a major rebuilding programme began which, over the next decade, saw the refurbishment of many of the now considerably aged locos. In the meantime, more new engines were purchased, beginning with a Hawthorn Leslie saddle tank No 3742 which arrived in 1929. This was followed by a further five saddle tanks from Peckett & Sons of Bristol as Nos 1811, 1837, 1966, 1932 and 1933, along with another Hawthorn Leslie, No 3794. All these appeared between 1930 and 1937.

Perhaps the arrival of the Pecketts instigated a cull of engines as no fewer than ten were disposed of in that period. Neilson No 3345 and HC No 287 went in 1930, MW No 457 in 1931, HL No 3742 went to Southall in 1932. Then Neilsons numbered 1659, 2227, 2228, 2380 all went in 1934, while Neilson No 3097 and AB No 262 disappeared in 1935. Following that exodus, 1938 saw the departure of the original Neilson No 1562 that had been rebuilt as Sentinel No 6951 and the same year marked the end of the line for Neilson No 2382 and HC No 657.

A new plant was installed in 1931 primarily for the production of coke, although the gas produced from it was also drawn off to the mains. The coke ovens were built at the southern part of the works where the hot coke was discharged into a 12-ton capacity wagon. To operate this, a new electric locomotive was purchased from Wellman Smith Owen of Darlaston, Staffordshire. This was No 1408 built in 1929 and the first of three from that maker that were to be employed at the ovens. The second, No 4191 built 1945, arrived when the ovens were extended in 1948. The locos ran on a short length of standard gauge track adjacent to the ovens and only one was in use at any time, the other being held in reserve as a standby engine.

There had been an unsuccessful experiment with diesel traction back in 1934 when an 85hp loco, No D23, built by Armstrong Whitworth, was tested at the gas works and also around the Products factory. However, it does seem that in an air of unpopularity with the steam crews, the experiment was somewhat loaded unfavourably against it. A train on a section of curved gradient was chosen for one trial and, this being infamous for stalling even the most robust steamers, proved too much for the interloper. Needless to say, it was deemed a failure and the status quo ruled for the succeeding decades. It then remained on less demanding duties for about a year before being sold to the Admiralty at Chatham Dockyard.

GLCC Beckton Gas Works 0-4-0ST Hunslet No 1335

Manufacturer:	Hunslet Engine Co Ltd
Built:	1919
Works number:	1335
Running number:	No 40
Cylinders:	12in x 18in
Driving Wheels:	3ft 1in
Wheelbase:	5ft 4in
Boiler pressure:	120psi
Weight:	20ton 8cwt
Length:	19ft 4in
Height:	9ft 8in
At Beckton Gas Works:	1919 – 1959

After taking on several second hand locomotives during WW1, peacetime saw a return to purchasing engines from new. Hunslet No 1335 arrived in December 1919 with conventional spring buffers and a cab but these were removed prior to it running as Beckton's No 40 and in 1928 it was recorded as working on the exchange sidings at Beckton Station. Its time at the Gas Works lasted June 1959 when it was scrapped there by merchants Drew and Sawyer of Belvedere in Kent.

Beckton's No 40 was Hunslet No 1335, seen here in an idle moment on 24th August 1957. (R C Riley/Transport Treasury)

GLCC Beckton Gas Works 2w-2PMR Baguley No 790

Manufacturer:	Baguley Cars Ltd
Built:	1920
Works number:	790
Engine:	25hp Baguley
Weight:	3ton 16cwt
At Beckton Gas Works:	1920 – 1930s

The unusual classification of this vehicle is due to it having the rear wheels driven by a petrol mechanical engine and being regarded as a railcar. In effect, this was not so much a locomotive but a lorry adapted with flanged wheels for transporting goods and personnel around the works railway system. It was sent new from the makers on 22nd July 1920 and not much else is recorded, but it is thought this, and a similar vehicle (Baguley No 1335), were disposed of by the late 1930s.

GLCC Beckton Gas Works 0-4-0T Barclay No 1720

Manufacturer:	Andrew Barclay Sons & Co Ltd
Built:	1921
Works number:	1720
Running number:	No 41 (No 4)
Cylinders:	12in x 18in
Driving Wheels:	3ft 0in
Wheelbase:	5ft 0in
Weight:	21ton 16cwt
Length:	19ft 6in
Height:	8ft 2in
At Beckton Gas Works:	1921 – 1961

Sent new from the makers on 3rd February 1921, Barclay No 1720 was one of a trio supplied from this maker on that date. It was given the running No 41, continuing the established sequence but, after the scrapping of MW No 457 in 1931, it carried the former engine's No 4. Its days at Beckton ended when disposed of for scrap in 1961.

GLCC Beckton Gas Works 0-4-0T Barclay No 1721

Manufacturer:	Andrew Barclay Sons & Co Ltd
Built:	1921
Works number:	1721
Running number:	No 42 (No 36)
Cylinders:	12in x 18in
Driving Wheels:	3ft 0in
Wheelbase:	5ft 0in
Weight:	20ton 13cwt
Length:	19ft 6in
Height:	8ft 2in
At Beckton Gas Works:	1921 – 1961

The second of three locos supplied to Beckton on 3rd February 1921, No 1721 was originally allocated running No 42 but became No 36, taking the place of the earlier holder that was transferred to Bromley-by-Bow in October the previous year. Like its sister No 1720 it remained in service until scrapped in 1961.

A rare glimpse of one of the two Beckton Baguley "locos" that were basically a lorry chassis adapted for rail operation. This is thought to be the earlier arrival, No 790, as it differs from the illustration of No 1335. (Peter Smith Collection)

Barclay No 1720 was originally allocated running No 41 but renumbered as No 4. (Industrial Locomotive Society Collection)

Barclay No 1721 in later guise as Beckton No 36 with a coke train on 2nd June 1956. (Reproduced by courtesy of the RCTS photo archive)

GLCC Beckton Gas Works 0-4-0T Barclay No 1722

Manufacturer:	Andrew Barclay Sons & Co Ltd
Built:	1921
Works number:	1722
Running number:	No 43 (No 39)
Cylinders:	12in x 18in
Driving Wheels:	3ft 0in
Wheelbase:	5ft 0in
Weight:	20ton 13cwt
Length:	19ft 6in
Height:	8ft 2in
At Beckton Gas Works:	1921 – 1960

Last of the three Barclays sent to Beckton on 3rd February 1921, when it was briefly numbered 43 before being allocated No 39, as replacement for an earlier loco that had been transferred to Bromley-by-Bow Gas Works. Although suffering damage in an air raid in January 1941 it continued working after repairs and lasted until being broken up on site by merchant H F A Dolman of Southend in November 1960.

GLCC Beckton Gas Works 2w-2PMR Baguley No 1335

Manufacturer:	Baguley Cars Ltd
Built:	1923
Works number:	1335
Engine:	25hp Baguley
Weight:	3ton 16cwt
At Beckton Gas Works:	1923 – 1930s

Another adapted road vehicle from Baguley, who had supplied No 790 in 1920. This one left their works on 5th October 1923 and performed the same duties as the earlier arrival. Both had a load capacity of two tons and, like its sister, it was probably disposed of in the late 1930s.

GLCC Beckton Gas Works 0-4-0VBT Sentinel No 6951

Manufacturer:	Sentinel (Shrewsbury) Ltd
Built:	1927 (Rebuilt by Sentinel from Neilson No 1562)
Works number:	S 6951
Running number:	No 2
Cylinders:	6.75in x 9in
Driving Wheels:	2ft 9in
Wheelbase:	5ft 0in
At Beckton Gas Works:	1927 – 1938 (Originally from 1870 – 1927 as Neilson No 1562)

This loco begin life at Beckton, having arrived as Neilson No 1562 in 1870. On 26th February 1927 the Sentinel Company was invited to rebuild it with parts of their own to produce locomotive No 6951. Sentinel specialised in vertical boilered geared tank engines and, although the frames and wheels of the Neilson were retained, the rest of the "hybrid" was of Sentinel origin. The work was carried out between May and October 1927 and Beckton No 2 emerged in its new form. The rebuild was not a success and compared unfavourably with the original loco, while the crews were unimpressed and referred to it as the "shoebox". Such was its unpopularity, it saw little further use before being disposed of in 1938.

Beckton's No 39 was Barclay No 1722. Having been allocated No 42 on arrival it was soon renumbered to fill a gap left by a previously transferred engine. (R C Riley/ Transport Treasury)

Beckton's second Baguley vehicle No 1335 was built in 1923 and differed slightly from the earlier model supplied to Beckton in 1920. (Industrial Railway Society Collection)

Neilson No 1562 began life as an identical sister to sister No 1561, but its appearance was dramatically altered after being rebuilt by Sentinel as a geared tank engine in 1927. It is seen here in its new outline. (Author's Collection)

GLCC Beckton Gas Works 0-4-0ST Hawthorn, Leslie No 3742

Manufacturer:	R & W Hawthorn, Leslie & Co Ltd
Built:	1929
Works number:	3742
Running number:	No 5
Cylinders:	14in x 22in
Driving Wheels:	3ft 6in
At Beckton Gas Works:	1929 – 1932

This was Beckton's first new locomotive since the three Barclays that had arrived in 1921. HL No 3742 was sent from the makers on 27th November 1929 and given the running No 5, vacant since the scrapping of No 2151 in 1927. It was one of the few Beckton engines to have a cab; however, it proved unsuitable and didn't stay long before being transferred to Southall Gas Works in 1932 where it worked on until scrapped in 1961.

GLCC Beckton Gas Works 0-4-0ST Peckett No 1811

Manufacturer:	Peckett & Son Ltd
Built:	1930
Works number:	1811
Running number:	No 15
Cylinders:	14in x 22in
Driving Wheels:	3ft 2.5in
Wheelbase:	5ft 0in
Boiler Pressure:	160psi
Weight:	29ton 3cwt
Length:	22ft 3ins
Height:	9ft 10ins
At Beckton Gas Works:	1930 – 1959

Turned out from Peckett's Bristol workshops on 16th June 1930, No 1811 was a special adaptation of the firm's W6 class and was the first of several larger engines to work the heavier coal and coke trains that resulted from revamped handling facilities. Taking the vacant No 15, it lasted until the dieselisation of Beckton was well established, being sold via dealers Drew & Sawyer to the firm of Lacmots Ltd in 1959 for export to Italy.

GLCC Beckton Gas Works 0-4-0WE Wellman Smith Owen No 1408

Manufacturer:	Wellman Smith Owen Engineering Corporation Ltd
Built:	1929
Works number:	1408
Weight:	15ton 0cwt
At Beckton Gas Works:	1931 – 1973

Delivered as new, this was the first of three specially designed locos built for use on an isolated section of track alongside the coke plant where it manoeuvred a 12 ton wagon in collecting hot coke from the ovens. In total there were three of these types but all were out of use by 1969 and dispensed with around 1973.

Hawthorn Leslie No 3742 was Beckton's second No 5, but its stay was short before being transferred to Southall Gas Works. (Industrial Locomotive Society Collection)

One of Beckton's biggest and heaviest locos was Peckett No 1811, a special build from that maker. It ran as No 15 and was pictured on 21st February 1953. (L R Freeman/Transport Treasury)

WSO No 1408, seen loading hot coke at the ovens. (WSO/Industrial Railway Society Collection)

GLCC Beckton Gas Works 0-4-0ST Peckett No 1837

Manufacturer:	Peckett & Son Ltd
Built:	1931
Works number:	1837
Running number:	No 37
Cylinders:	14in x 22in
Driving Wheels:	3ft 2.5in
Wheelbase:	5ft 0in
Boiler Pressure:	160psi
Weight:	28ton 2cwt
Length:	22ft 3ins
Height:	9ft 10ins
At Beckton Gas Works:	1931 – 1962

The second heavyweight Peckett was sent to Beckton on 20th October 1931, taking over No 37 from the scrapped HC No 287. It lasted until disposed of in 1962 when a purge of engines took place following the introduction of diesel locomotives during the previous three years.

GLCC Beckton Gas Works 0-4-0ST Hawthorn, Leslie No 3794

Manufacturer:	R & W Hawthorn, Leslie & Co Ltd
Built:	1931
Works number:	3794
Running number:	No 5
Cylinders:	14in x 22in
Driving Wheels:	3ft 4in
Wheelbase:	5ft 6in
Boiler Pressure:	160psi
Weight:	26ton 0cwt
Length:	21ft 10in
Height:	9ft 4ins
At Beckton Gas Works:	1932 – 1959

One of only two Beckton Gas Works locos supplied by Hawthorn, Leslie, No 3794 was completed by the makers on 19th November 1931. It was purchased as a replacement for its sister engine No 3742, which was due for transfer to Southall Gas Works in early 1932. It also took its predecessor's running number and became Beckton's third No 5 until becoming one of several locos broken up on site in June 1959 by merchants Drew & Sawyer of Belvedere, Kent.

GLCC Beckton Gas Works 0-4-0DE Armstrong, Whitworth No D23

Name:	*(Walmer Castle)*
Manufacturer:	Sir W G Armstrong, Whitworth & Co Ltd
Built:	1933
Works number:	D23
Engine:	85hp Saurer 6BLD
At Beckton Gas Works:	1934

Beckton's early experimentation with diesel traction in 1934 proved less than successful as Armstrong Whitworth's No D23 was sent on 7th June that year. It had something of a hostile reception by resident steam crews and was given tasks that were more demanding than most everyday requirements. It remained on site performing lesser duties for several months before being sent to Chatham Dockyard in Kent where it carried the name *Walmer Castle*, working there until scrapped in March 1966.

Beckton Gas Works: Gas Light & Coke Company 1902-1949

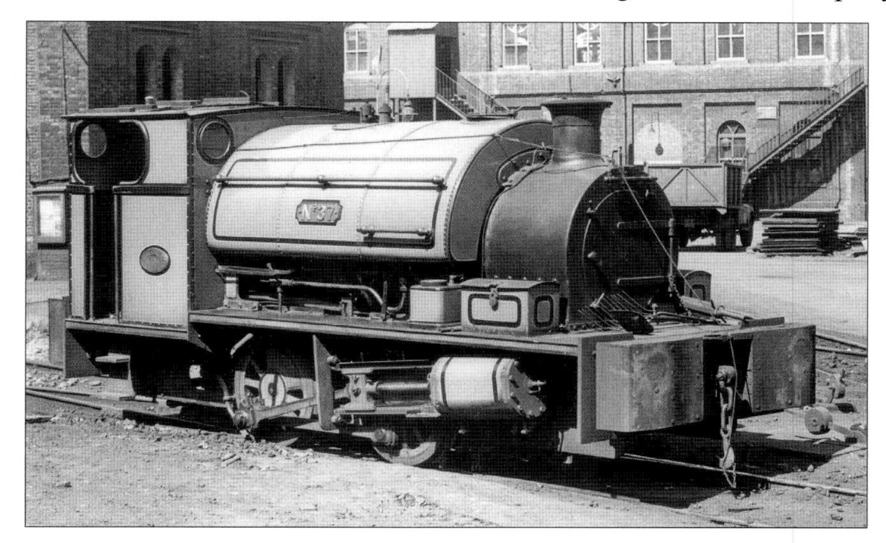

No 1837 was Beckton's second heavy-duty Peckett, and worked until 1962 when it became a casualty of the railway's change to diesel traction. (Douglas Clayton Collection/Industrial Railway Society)

Beckton's second Hawthorn, Leslie engine was No 3794 seen here on 24th August 1957. It also became No 5, which was the running number of its predecessor No 3742, following that loco's transfer to Southall Gas Works. (R C Riley, Transport Treasury)

Armstrong, Whitworth No D23 was an early diesel trialist at Beckton, but was soon redeployed at Chatham Dockyard where it was photographed on 24th September 1962. (Brian Webb Collection/ Industrial Railway Society)

GLCC Beckton Gas Works 0-4-0ST Peckett No 1932

Manufacturer:	Peckett & Sons Ltd
Built:	1937
Works number:	1932
Running number:	No 3
Cylinders:	14in x 22in
Driving Wheels:	3ft 2.5in
Wheelbase:	5ft 0in
Boiler Pressure:	160psi
Weight:	28ton 19cwt
Length:	22ft 3in
Height:	9ft 10in
At Beckton Gas Works:	1937 – 1959

Another of Beckton's "heavy brigade", Peckett No 1932 was another adaptation of the maker's W6 class engine when sent new from their workshops on 7th July 1937. After little more than a couple of decades at the Gas Works it joined sister Peckett No 1811 on a trip to Italy after being sold to Lascmots Ltd, via agents Drew & Sawyer, in 1959.

GLCC Beckton Gas Works 0-4-0ST Peckett No 1933

Manufacturer:	Peckett & Sons Ltd
Built:	1937
Works number:	1933
Running number:	No 6
Cylinders:	14in x 22in
Driving Wheels:	3ft 2.5in
Wheelbase:	5ft 0in
Boiler Pressure:	160psi
Weight:	28ton 19cwt
Length:	22ft 3in
Height:	9ft 10in
At Beckton Gas Works:	1937 – 1960

No 1933 was another special build of Peckett's W6 class engine and left their works on 9th August 1937 for Beckton. Working until 1960 it became one of five locos broken up by George Cohen, Sons & Co in May that year.

A nicely turned out Peckett No 1932 poses for the camera outside Beckton's roundhouse shed. (Douglas Clayton Collection/Industrial Railway Society)

Peckett No 1933 pictured at Beckton Gas Works on 30th October 1954. (J B Latham/ Industrial Locomotive Society)

Seen here inside the Roundhouse Shed, Peckett No 1966 became one of Beckton's last working steam locos, running until being disposed of in 1967. (Industrial Locomotive Society Collection)

GLCC Beckton Gas Works 0-4-0ST Peckett No 1966

Manufacturer:	Peckett & Sons Ltd
Built:	1939
Works number:	1966
Running number:	No 2
Cylinders:	12in x 18in
Driving Wheels:	3ft 0in
Wheelbase:	5ft 0in
Boiler Pressure:	160psi
Weight:	20ton 0cwt
Length:	20ft 2in
Height:	9ft 6in
At Beckton Gas Works:	1939 – 1967

Beckton's third Peckett loco arrived in 1939 after leaving the builders on 15th March that year, being a special adaptation of their R2 class engine. It replaced the unpopular Sentinel rebuild of Neilson No 1562 and took its running No 2, working at the gas works and becoming one of the last remaining steamers when scrapped in February 1967. (See page 61 for an illustration of this loco.)

During the WW2 blitz, a bombing raid in January 1941 resulted in damage to a number of the gas works locos, in particular BH 864 (No 18), N 5086 (No 24) AB 636 (No 33) and AB 1722 (No 39). All were sent away for repair, possibly to the firm of Colishaw Walker, and some replacements were taken on loan from the LNER in that year, including Sentinel Nos 78 and 87. Further reinforcements were called upon in the shape of two saddle tanks from W G Bagnall of Stafford. These were Nos 2657 and 2658 arriving new in 1942.

During the war years, night time blackouts were imposed to discourage enemy bombing and the large windows of the mostly glazed Beckton workshops were sheeted over with galvanised iron.

An additional engine arrived immediately after the war, this was a Manning Wardle saddle tank No 1427 dating from 1899 that had been rebuilt several times, latterly by Hudswell Clarke in 1945. A Hudswell Clarke original, No 522, was purchased second hand in 1947. The next arrival was a Robert Stephenson & Hawthorn engine supplied new in 1949 as No 7474. This was the last Beckton locomotive purchased by the Gas Light and Coke Company before the works came under the authority of the North Thames Gas Board from 1st May 1949.

One of the original pair of Neilson locos (No 1562) was rebuilt by Sentinel in 1927 but the result proved both unsatisfactory and unpopular. (Jim Peden Collection/Industrial Railway Society)

Beckton Gas Works: Gas Light & Coke Company 1902-1949

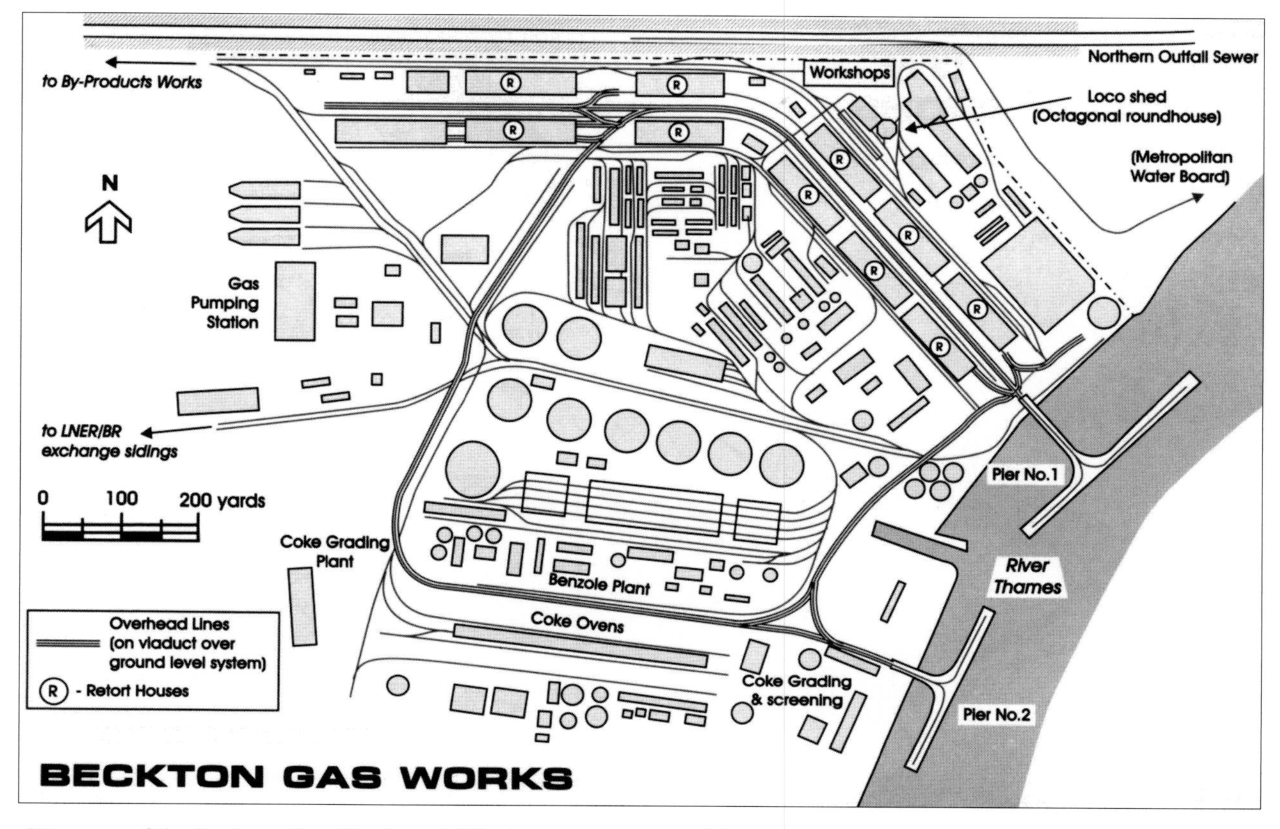

Diagram of the Beckton Gas Works in 1938 showing the general layout and main buildings. (Map by Roger Hateley)

The Gas Works and Products Factory locos often met on common ground. On the left No 1561 (No 1) with No 1659 (No 3) in the foreground while No 4444 (No 1) is in the background in this scene from the 1930s. (Industrial Locomotive Society Collection)

The Beckton maintenance workshops where manufacturing, repairs and painting of railway stock was a continuous process. During WWII the large glazed areas were blacked out with sheets of galvanised iron. (Industrial Locomotive Society Collection)

Beckton Gas Works seen from the Northern Outfall in the latter days of the GLCC. The Roundhouse shed is at the centre of the photo while the Maintenance Workshops on the right dominate the scene. Running left to right across the foreground is an embankment with the remains of the former narrow gauge line that ran from the adjacent London County Council sewage works (see Chapter 9). (Industrial Locomotive Society Collection)

GLCC Beckton Gas Works 0-4-0ST Bagnall No 2657

Manufacturer:	W G Bagnall Ltd
Built:	1942
Works number:	2657
Running number:	No 7
Cylinders:	12in x 18in
Driving Wheels:	2ft 9in
Wheelbase:	5ft 0in
Boiler Pressure:	160psi
Weight:	20ton 0cwt
Length:	20ft 2in
Height:	9ft 8in
At Beckton Gas Works:	1942 – 1967

World War Two saw the arrival of two purchases from W G Bagnall in 1942. Nos 2657 and 2658 were both completed on 23rd March that year and dispatched to Beckton. No 2657 survived the longest of the pair, working until scrapped in February 1967.

Beckton's first loco supplied from makers W G Bagnall pictured at the gas works with contemporaries on 12th April 1958. (L R Freeman/Transport Treasury)

GLCC Beckton Gas Works 0-4-0ST Bagnall No 2658

Manufacturer:	W G Bagnall Ltd
Built:	1942
Works number:	2658
Running number:	No 8
Cylinders:	12in x 18in
Driving Wheels:	2ft 9in
Wheelbase:	5ft 0in
Boiler Pressure:	160psi
Weight:	20ton 1cwt
Length:	20ft 2in
Height:	9ft 8in
At Beckton Gas Works:	1942 – 1961

The second of two wartime arrivals from Bagnall, purchased new in 1942, However, No 2658 lasted several years less than its twin, having been broken up in 1961.

GLCC Beckton Gas Works 0-4-0ST Manning Wardle No 1427

Manufacturer:	Manning Wardle & Co Ltd
Built:	1899
Works number:	1427
Running number:	No 9
Cylinders:	14in x 18in
Driving Wheels:	3ft 0in
Wheelbase:	5ft 6in
Boiler Pressure:	140psi
Weight:	23ton 5cwt
Length:	22ft 0in
Height:	10ft 3in
Water capacity:	550gals
At Beckton Gas Works:	1946 – 1959

This Manning Wardle P class engine built with special frames was completed on 8th February 1899 and delivered to the Burton Brewery Company, running as their No 4 loco. In 1916 it was rebuilt by the makers and returned to the brewery where it remained until sold to the Mansfield Standard Sand Co Ltd at Nottingham in 1926. In 1945 it was again rebuilt, this time by Hudswell Clarke who then sold the loco to Beckton Gas Works the following year. With an overall height of 10ft 3in it was the tallest loco to work at Beckton and continued in service until scrapped on site by merchants Drew and Sawyer in June 1959.

Bagnall No 2658 in the long shed with RSH No 7474 at the rear on 2nd April 1959. Note the Westinghouse air pump beside the smokebox for operating the doors on hopper wagons such as the one on the right. (Sydney A Leleux)

MW No 1427 at work on 22nd April 1959; its days were already numbered and ended just two months later. (Sydney A Leleux)

The much travelled HC No 522 running as Beckton No 38 on 30th October 1954. (Reproduced by courtesy of the RCTS photo archive)

GLCC Beckton Gas Works 0-4-0ST Hudswell, Clarke No 522

Name:	*(Covenanter), (Nonsuch)*
Manufacturer:	Hudswell, Clarke & Co Ltd
Built:	1899
Works number:	522
Running number:	No 38
Cylinders:	9in x 15in
Driving Wheels:	2ft 9in
Wheelbase:	5ft 0in
Boiler Pressure:	160psi
Weight:	13ton 0cwt
Length:	16ft 6in
Height:	8ft 2in
At Beckton Gas Works:	1947 – 1958

No 522 was completed on 29th March 1899 and sent to contractor Sir Robert McAlpine carrying the name *Covenanter* at a cost of £740.00. It worked on the construction of the Lanarkshire & Ayrshire Railway until 1904 and was afterwards thought to have been used in the building of Methil Dock. It was at McAlpine's Great Stanney depot in 1921 and listed for scrapping in 1926 but was instead sold to the Wandsworth & District Gas Company, at Kingston-on-Thames, Surrey, where it was named *Nonsuch*. By March 1947 it had been purchased by the GLCC at Beckton Gas Works where it took the vacant No 38 that had previously been carried by another Hudswell Clarke engine, No 657, working on until scrapped by George Cohen, Sons & Co in August 1958. (See page 67 for an illustration of this loco.)

GLCC Beckton Gas Works 0-4-0WE Wellman Smith Owen No 4191

Manufacturer:	Wellman Smith Owen Engineering Corporation Ltd
Built:	1945
Works number:	4191
Engine:	80hp
At Beckton Gas Works:	1948 – 1973

The second of three locos commissioned for work at the Beckton coke ovens arrived as new in 1948 but like its sisters worked only until 1969 and was scrapped in 1973

GLCC Beckton Gas Works 0-4-0ST RSH No 7474

Manufacturer:	Robert Stephenson & Hawthorns Ltd
Built:	1949
Works number:	7474
Running number:	No 14
Cylinders:	12in x 20in
Driving Wheels:	3ft 0in
Wheelbase:	5ft 0in
Boiler Pressure:	160psi
Weight:	21ton 17cwt
Length:	20ft 0in
Height:	10ft 4in
At Beckton Gas Works:	1949 – 1962

This was the only RSH saddle tank loco to grace the rails at Beckton, although two fireless engines from the same maker arrived later. No 7474 was turned out of the Newcastle Workshops on 24th January 1949 and became Beckton No 14, a number that had been vacant since the scrapping of Neilson No 3097 in 1935. This loco was delivered with a cab and became the final locomotive purchased by the GLCC before the industry was nationalised. Its cab was removed in 1955 and its time at the gas works was relatively short, lasting only thirteen years before being scrapped in 1962.

Another of the three WSO locos at work alongside the Beckton Coke Ovens. (Peter Smith Collection)

Beckton's only RSH saddle tank loco No 7474 was the last engine acquired by the GLCC before nationalisation of the industry, and is seen at the gas works on 22nd April 1959. Behind and to the right is Peckett No 2123. (Sydney A Leleux)

Beckton's Railways and Locomotives

Summary of Gas Works Locos Purchased by Gas Light & Coke Company						
Maker	**Works No**	**Date Built**	**Type**	**Running No**	**Date Arrived**	**Date Departed**
N	1561	1870	0-4-0WT	1	1870	1963
N	1562	1870	0-4-0WT	2	1870	1927*
N	1659	1872	0-4-0WT	3	1872	1934
Chap	1675	1874	0-4-0VBT	1	1874	c1900
Chap	1756	1874	0-4-0VBT	2	1874	c1900
Chap	1757	1874	0-4-0VBT	3	1874	c1900
MW	457	1875	0-4-0ST	4	1875	1931
N	2151	1876	0-4-0WT	5	1876	1927
N	2227	1877	0-4-0WT	6	1877	1934
N	2228	1877	0-4-0WT	7	1877	1934
N	2380	1878	0-4-0WT	8	1878	1934
N	2382	1878	0-4-0T	9	1878	1938
N	2465	1879	0-4-0T	10	1879	1962
N	2466	1879	0-4-0T	11	1879	1961
N	2597	1880	0-4-0T	12	1880	1960
N	2598	1880	0-4-0T	13	1880	1967
N	3097	1883	0-4-0ST	14	1883	1935
N	3345	1884	0-4-0ST	15	1884	1930
N	3451	1885	0-4-0ST	16	1885	1958
BH	865	1886	0-4-0ST	17	1886	1958
BH	864	1886	0-4-0T	18	1886	1959
N	3789	1888	0-4-0T	19	1888	1962
N	4249	1890	0-4-0T	20	1890	1960
N	4250	1890	0-4-0ST	21	1890	1959
N	4414	1891	0-4-0T	22	1891	1960
N	4408	1892	0-4-0T	23	1892	1967
N	5086	1896	0-4-0T	24	1896	1958
N	5087	1896	0-4-0ST	25	1896	1961
N	5228	1897	0-4-0T	26	1897	1960
N	5229	1897	0-4-0T	27	1897	1962
N	5230	1897	0-4-0T	28	1897	1962
N	5231	1897	0-4-0T	29	1897	1962
Beckton	1	1902	0-4-0T	30	1902	1960
Beckton	2	1902	0-4-0T	31	1902	1959
MW	901	1885	0-4-0ST	32	1909	1912
MW	1832	1913	0-4-0ST	32	1913	1955
AB	636	1889	0-4-0ST	33	1916	1949
AB	262	1883	0-4-0ST	34	1916	1935
AB	957	1902	0-4-0ST	35	1917	1949
AB	266	1884	0-4-0ST	36	1917	1918
HC	657	1903	0-4-0ST	38	1918	1938
AB	?	?	0-4-0ST	39	1918	1920
HC	287	1887	0-4-0ST	37	1919	1930
HE	1335	1919	0-4-0ST	40	1919	1959
BgC	790	1920	2w-2PMR	n/a	1920	1930s
AB	1720	1921	0-4-0T	41 (4)	1921	1961
AB	1721	1921	0-4-0T	42 (36)	1921	1961
AB	1722	1921	0-4-0T	43 (39)	1921	1960
BgC	1335	1923	2w-2PMR	n/a	1923	1930s
S	6951	1927	0-4-0VBT	2	1927*	1938
HL	3742	1929	0-4-0ST	5	1929	1932
P	1811	1930	0-4-0ST	15	1930	1959
WSO	1408	1929	0-4-0WE	n/a	1931	1973
P	1837	1931	0-4-0ST	37	1931	1962
HL	3794	1931	0-4-0ST	5	1932	1959
AW	D23	1933	0-4-0DE	n/a	1934	1934
P	1932	1937	0-4-0ST	3	1937	1959
P	1933	1937	0-4-0ST	6	1937	1960
P	1966	1939	0-4-0ST	2	1939	1967
WB	2657	1942	0-4-0ST	7	1942	1967
WB	2658	1942	0-4-0ST	8	1942	1961
MW	1427	1899	0-4-0ST	9	1946	1959
HC	522	1899	0-4-0ST	38	1947	1958
WSO	4191	1945	0-4-0WE	n/a	1948	1973
RSH	7474	1949	0-4-0ST	14	1949	1962
* Loco rebuilt as S 6951 in 1927						

CHAPTER 3

Beckton Gas Works

The Gas Light & Coke Company Passenger Vehicles

Quite apart from the multitude of internal coal, coke and clinker wagons, the GLCC had several types of passenger vehicle for the transportation of personnel and VIPs around the vast works. These included a number a four-wheeled glazed wagons, possibly used as observation cars, at least four small coaches, one of which was used as a travelling pay office, plus one rather grand passenger carriage, built in 1860 for the Eastern Counties Railway, which later became a constituent of the Great Eastern Railway. This was reserved for transporting VIPs around the site. One such prodigious occasion was a visit by King George V and Queen Mary, who were given a tour of the works on 10th July 1926. Sadly, in September 1940, the carriage was damaged in an air raid and never used again. As for the others, there seem to have been very few sightings of these in the days of the NTGB.

Left: *One of the Beckton passenger stock, a four wheeled observation car, with Neilson No 4408 (No 23) in charge on 9th July 1927. (H C Casserley)*

Below: *The "Royal Train", reserved for VIPs, photographed on 9th July 1927 with the plush carriage headed by an immaculate No 30, Beckton built No 1. (H C Casserley)*

Beckton's pride of fleet No 31 (Beckton built No 2) is seen here having ventured into the Products Works with one of the personnel coaches on 9th June 1934. (H F Wheeller Collection)

Another fine study of the "Royal Train" on parade at Beckton Gas works. (Frank Jones)

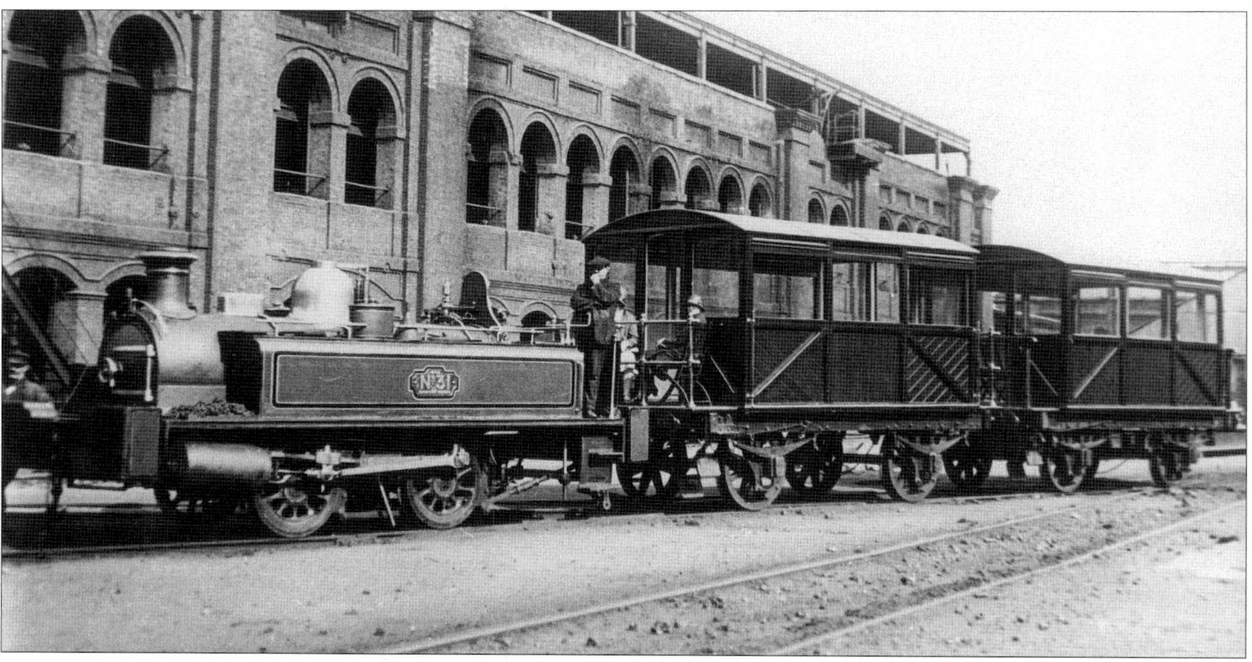

No 31 again, this time with a pair of glazed carriages. (Courtesy of Newham Heritage and Archives)

Two Neilson hauled trains, with a collection of passenger stock, stand on one of the Beckton piers, possibly for a visit of VIPs, but there appear to be class distinctions with glazed coaches and converted open wagons from the LNER, suitably adapted with benches and awnings. (Peter Smith Collection)

Flags flutter on the occasion of a Royal visit to Beckton on 10th July 1926 as No 31 hauls the Royal Party along No 1 Pier on a tour of the new coal handling facilities installed that year. For this special event, the loco was fitted with a taller chimney to ensure that any smoke would be carried above the VIP carriage. HRH King George V can be seen peering through the left hand window. (Peter Smith Collection)

Two passenger trains together on the upper level, passing under the signal box at No 1 Pier on 9th July 1927, consisting of Neilson No 4408, with an observation car and No 30 (Beckton-built No 1) handling the VIP carriage. (H C Casserley)

CHAPTER 4

Beckton Gas Works

The North Thames Gas Board 1949-1970

Upon the nationalisation of the industry, the gas companies were replaced by regional boards and Beckton came under the umbrella of the North Thames Gas Board on 1st May 1949. The new administration inherited some 41 locos from its predecessor, including the first Neilson No 1561 and the two locos built by Beckton's own workshops.

Summary of Gas Works locos acquired by North Thames Gas Board in 1949

Maker	Works No	Date Built	Type	Running No	Date Arrived	Date Departed
N	1561	1870	0-4-0WT	1	1870	1963
N	2465	1879	0-4-0T	10	1879	1962
N	2466	1879	0-4-0T	11	1879	1961
N	2597	1880	0-4-0T	12	1880	1960
N	2598	1880	0-4-0T	13	1880	1967
N	3451	1885	0-4-0ST	16	1885	1958
BH	865	1886	0-4-0ST	17	1886	1958
BH	864	1886	0-4-0T	18	1886	1959
N	3789	1888	0-4-0T	19	1888	1962
N	4249	1890	0-4-0T	20	1890	1960
N	4250	1890	0-4-0ST	21	1890	1959
N	4414	1891	0-4-0T	22	1891	1960
N	4408	1892	0-4-0T	23	1892	1967
N	5086	1896	0-4-0T	24	1896	1958
N	5087	1896	0-4-0ST	25	1896	1961
N	5228	1897	0-4-0T	26	1897	1960
N	5229	1897	0-4-0T	27	1897	1962
N	5230	1897	0-4-0T	28	1897	1962
N	5231	1897	0-4-0T	29	1897	1962
Beckton	1	1902	0-4-0T	30	1902	1960
Beckton	2	1902	0-4-0T	31	1902	1959
MW	1832	1913	0-4-0ST	32	1913	1955
AB	636	1889	0-4-0ST	33	1916	1949
AB	957	1902	0-4-0ST	35	1917	1949
HE	1335	1919	0-4-0ST	40	1919	1959
AB	1720	1921	0-4-0T	4 (41)	1921	1961
AB	1721	1921	0-4-0T	36 (42)	1921	1961
AB	1722	1921	0-4-0T	39 (43)	1921	1960
P	1811	1930	0-4-0ST	15	1930	1959
WSO	1408	1929	0-4-0WE	n/a	1931	1973
P	1837	1931	0-4-0ST	37	1931	1962
HL	3794	1931	0-4-0ST	5	1932	1959
P	1932	1937	0-4-0ST	3	1937	1959
P	1933	1937	0-4-0ST	6	1937	1960
P	1966	1939	0-4-0ST	2	1939	1967
WB	2657	1942	0-4-0ST	7	1942	1967
WB	2658	1942	0-4-0ST	8	1942	1961
MW	1427	1899	0-4-0ST	9	1946	1959
HC	522	1899	0-4-0ST	38	1947	1958
WSO	4191	1945	0-4-0WE	n/a	1948	1973
RSH	7474	1949	0-4-0ST	14	1949	1962

Following nationalisation, the two Barclay engines (Nos 636 and 957) were disposed of in 1949 and the North Thames Gas Board began to look at modernising the Beckton loco fleet by dieselisation. Another consideration was the firm of Sentinel that specialised in vertical boilered geared tank locos, and they sent one of their engines to the gas works to demonstrate its capabilities. This was their 100hp No 9398, new from 1st January 1950 and it initially proved impressive (unlike their earlier rebuild of Neilson No 1652 back in 1927). The loco was put through it paces in October 1951 but it was adjudged not to be commercially advantageous over the existing steamers and sent back to its makers.

Instead, two more steam locos were obtained new from separate makers. Peckett No 2123 proved to be the final saddle tank arrival at Beckton Gas Works and was also its last coal-fired engine. The other was a Robert Stephenson & Hawthorn fireless loco, No 7665 which was followed by a sister loco, No 7803, in 1954. These were both designed for work in areas that were prone to fire risk, in particular around the works purifying plant where flammable gasses were present.

From 1955 until 1957 the firm of Holloway Brothers Ltd was engaged to rebuild the gas works river wall along the Thames at a cost of £519,000. During those works they employed a standard gauge 4wDM Hibberd loco No FH 3700/1955 and three 2ft 0in gauge 4wDM Motor Rail locos, all built in 1948.

Following a post war boom in demand, and the effect of Clean Air Acts, production from the coke ovens was expanded in 1956 and a third electric loco arrived at the Gas Works. This was another WSO built engine, No 5785 of 1953, becoming the last of a trio that took turns of duty until the plant ceased production in 1969.

MW No 1832 had gone by 1955 so by March 1957 there were 37 steam, two fireless and three electric locos employed at the works. Extensive alterations to the ground level rail layout took place in 1958 with coke levels at their peak, after which outgoing coke trains were assembled at a new yard inside the works, rather than the sidings at the station. At the same time, the signalling system was completely overhauled with the old semaphores being replaced by fully automated coloured lights that were now all controlled from a new central box which covered both overhead and ground level tracks.

A report commissioned in that year compared likely operating costs between steam and diesel traction. It concluded

The Coming Year

A Message from the Governor

DEAR CO-PARTNERS,

In sending you my best wishes for 1949 I cannot help being conscious of the fact that we must expect the coming year to mark for us the end of the Gas Light and Coke Company. I do not believe that the New Year is a time for looking back—except that by doing so it may be possible to benefit from our experience. In turning, therefore, to the coming year and to the future generally, I should like to say, not only for myself but for the Deputy Governor, Mr. F. M. Birks, that having accepted the Government's invitation to become Chairman and Deputy Chairman of the North Thames Gas Board, we shall do our utmost to continue the policy of the old Gas Light and Coke Company.

You all know full well what this policy is, because it has in the past received your enthusiastic support. First, to supply gas as cheaply as possible and to give good service to all our consumers. Second, fair treatment to every member of the Company. Provided that these two principles become the foundation of the North Thames Gas Board, as they have been of the Gas Light and Coke Company, I see no reason why we should not continue to enjoy the high reputation which the Gas Light and Coke Company has always held in the industry.

For this to happen, however, each one of us must realise that it is upon his or her own personal efforts that the success of the whole depends. For us the political issue of nationalisation is finished. Our task now is to forget politics and to get on with the job of providing Greater London north of the Thames with the best gas service in the world.

A very Happy New Year to you all.

Yours sincerely,

GOVERNOR

Left: *The beginning of a new era with the nationalisation of the gas industry had raised some misgivings within the Beckton workforce. In his message through the house magazine "Co-Partners" in January 1949, the Governor sought to reassure them that things would remain the same as in the old GLCC days. (Industrial Locomotive Society Collection)*

On the day of its arrival, the 30th June 1954, an immaculate RSH fireless loco No 7803 receives its Beckton buffer beam, supported by crane and manoeuvred into position by the local workforce. (J F Bruton/Industrial Locomotive Society Collection)

that 25 diesels could effectively replace the 37 steam engines, and this saw the beginning of the change to dieselisation from 1958 after steam had ruled for almost eight decades.

A Ruston & Hornsby loco No 421416 was taken on trial that year . It was transferred to Lea Bridge Gas Works after proving unsuccessful against others from the firm of F C Hibberd at Park Royal, London. Their 117hp "Planet" locos impressed and an initial pair were placed on order. Arriving in August 1958, FH Nos 3885 and 3889 were so successful that another six were requested in February 1959 and Nos 3907, 3908, 3909, 3910, 3911 and 3912 arrived in batches through the rest of that year. All the new diesel locos received the same green livery and Beckton-style number plates as their steam predecessors.

Their main dimensions of the Hibberd diesels are:

Driving wheels:	3ft 1.5in
Wheelbase:	5ft 6in
Engine:	117hp Dorman 6DL
Weight:	23ton 0cwt
Length:	18ft 2.5in
Height:	10ft 7in

By 1960, the loco fleet comprised nineteen steam engines, two fireless, three electric and eight diesels, while a final three Hibberds, Nos 3959, 3960 and 3961 were purchased in 1961, bringing the total to eleven. But these were not quite the final locos to arrive at the Gas Works as two steam engines, Peckett No 1574 and Neilson No 4571, were transferred on loan from the Products Factory in 1965 and 1966 respectively.

The entrance to Beckton gas works viewed from Winsor Terrace, looking east towards the level crossing gates on 4th October 1958. The car is a 1934 Hillman Minx belonging to the photographer. (H C Casserley)

Photographer Richard Casserley joined a party of invited guests who toured the works on 4th October 1958 and the occasion produced a series of images showing the upper levels of the rail system. Transportation for the party was in two open wagons hauled by Neilson No 5231 (Beckton No 29). The following four photographs record the excursion:

The tour party train on Beckton's No 1 Pier.

The driver's view from Neilson No 5231, heading from Pier No 1 on the overhead railway.

Looking down the "main line" on the Gas Works overhead railway, showing the openings in the track for depositing coal and coke into stock-piles below at ground level.

Another view from Neilson No 5231 showing the construction of elevated railway and its supporting columns.

Full steam ahead as loco No 21 (Neilson No 4250), with a train of coal for the upper level, takes a run at one of the inclines on 4th October 1958. (H C Casserley)

A classic shed scene outside the Beckton Roundhouse with Neilson No 5087 (No 25) manoeuvring a trio of its workmates. (Douglas Clayton Collection/Industrial Railway Society)

Locos inside the Long Shed on 4th October 1958 include P No 1932 (No 3), WB No 2658 (No 8), P No 2123 (No 33) and WB No 2657 (No 7). (H C Casserley)

Neilson No 5231 photographed at Beckton as it pauses for the camera on 4th October 1958. This loco ended its days at the adjacent Products Works. (R M Casserley)

Beckton Gas Works No 22, another of the heavier Neilson locos (No 4414) with extended side tanks, is pictured on 24th August 1957. (R C Riley/Transport Treasury)

Neilson No 5231 propels a party of visitors on a tour of the works in 1958. It is pictured on the upper level on 4th October that year. (H C Casserley)

Neilson No 3789 was an 1888 arrival at Beckton and is seen here with a coke train on 22nd April 1959. (Sydney A Leleux)

Bagnall No 2657, as Beckton No 7, on the overhead railway, with a train of coal hopper wagons, leaves No 1 Pier heading towards the 6000 ton bunker on 30th November 1957. (Chris Gammell/Photos from the Fifties)

Peckett No 1966 (Beckton No 2) stands by the 6000 ton coal bunker on 30th May 1960. The notice warns that no trains of fewer than 16 wagons should be loaded by the automatic system, as any shorter trains would result in coal being discharged on to the track! (R C Riley/Transport Treasury)

The arrival of the diesels saw a run down of the steam fleet, with Neilson Nos 3451 and 5086, Black Hawthorn No 865 and Hudswell, Clark No 522 all disposed of in 1958. Worse was to come in 1959 when BH No 864, Neilson No 4250, Beckton No 2, HE No 1335, Peckett Nos 1881 and 1932, HL No 3794 and MW No 1437 all went. 1960 was little better with the final appearances of Neilson Nos 2597, 4249, 4414, 5228, Beckton No 1, AB No 1722 and Peckett No 1933. 1961 said farewell to Neilson Nos 2466 and 5087, Barclay Nos 1720 and 1721, along with Bagnall No 2658.

By 1962 there were only eight steam locos remaining, plus the two fireless locos and the three electric at the coke plant, with the redundant engines being stored on sidings adjacent to the Long Shed while awaiting their fate. These were Neilson Nos 2465, 3789, 5229, 5230 and 5231, Peckett Nos 1837 and 2123, and RSH No 7474, which all met their end during that year. The exodus then halted for five years, apart from the departure of the original Neilson loco No 1561, retiring as Gas Works No 1, which was taken into preservation in 1963. Coincidentally, the Roundhouse Shed, which had stood since 1875, was demolished in that year.

A new gas main had been laid from Romford Gas Works into Beckton by 1959 and the mid 1960s saw the arrival of natural gas from the North Sea. Due to that competition, gas production at Beckton was dramatically reduced and there was also an effect on the Products Works. Because of this, rail movements overall were substantially reduced and moves were made to consolidate the two loco fleets. This proved difficult as each was run under different working conditions and rates of pay but this was gradually overcome and the final years of operation saw some locos from each stable working on its neighbours territory. Neilson Nos 2598 and 5231 and RSH No 7474 ventured into the Products Works, while Neilson No 4571 and Peckett No 1574 came in the opposite direction.

The few surviving remnants of the Beckton steam age said goodbye in 1967 when Neilson Nos 2598 and 4408, Peckett No 1966 and Bagnall No 2657 all disappeared.

As production at Beckton dwindled, the fleet of

Hibberd diesels was now becoming obsolete after a mere decade of employment and all of them, being mechanically sound, were found new homes. Nos 3885, 3889, 3907, and 3910 all departed in 1968. Nos 3908 and 3911 left in 1969, while Nos 3909, 3912, 3959 and 3960 were gone in 1970.

Gas production had finally ceased on 16th June 1969 and Beckton's final train left from the Products Works on 1st July 1970, leaving just Hibberd No 3961 and the two fireless locos, RSH Nos 7665 and 7803. The Hibberd went in 1971, as did RSH No 7665, while RSH No 7803 lingered on until 1972. The three coke oven locos were the final disposals in 1973, marking the end of a century of rail operations at Beckton.

In its latter years the site was managed by British Gas and Transco, but left in a neglected state, during which time it was often used as a place for film locations. Over its existence, the works had built up a huge mountain of waste that became known as the Beckton Alps. This was ultimately landscaped and redeveloped as a ski slope. Apart from a few derelict buildings, this landmark is now the only remnant of the former giant gasworks, part of which has now been redeveloped as a retail park, while, to the south, is the main depot of the Docklands Light Railway.

NTGB Beckton Gas Works 4wVBT Sentinel No 9398

Manufacturer:	Sentinel (Shrewsbury) Ltd
Built:	1950
Works number:	9398
Cylinders:	6.75in x 9in
Driving Wheels:	2ft 6in
At Beckton Gas Works:	1951

The gas industry had been nationalised on 1st May 1949 and the North Thames Gas Board was considering alternatives to the steam locos they had in their fleet. The firm of Sentinel sent one of their vertical boilered geared tank engines to Beckton to demonstrate its capabilities. This was their 100hp No 9398, new from 1st January 1950, which initially proved more impressive than their 1927 rebuild of Neilson No 1562. In October 1951 it was taken on trial but not considered as a viable alternative to the pending possible dieselisation and was returned to its makers within a few weeks.

NTGB Beckton Gas Works 0-4-0ST Peckett No 2123

Manufacturer:	Peckett & Sons Ltd
Built:	1951
Works number:	2123
Running number:	No 33
Cylinders:	12in x 18in
Driving Wheels:	2ft 9in
Wheelbase:	5ft 0in
Boiler pressure:	160psi
Weight:	20ton 0cwt
Length:	20ft 2in
Height:	9ft 6in
At Beckton Gas Works:	1951 – 1962

With dieselisation put on hold, the new regime at Beckton returned to steam for their first purchase of a new loco. This was Peckett No 2123, a special build of their R2 class which was ex works on 30th April 1951, taking the No 33 which had previously been carried by AB No 636. This was the last coal-fired engine to arrive at Beckton and, when the takeover by diesels finally came, this was one of a number of steamers scrapped in 1962. (This loco is illustrated on Page 87.)

NTGB Beckton Gas Works 0-4-0F RSH No 7665

Manufacturer:	Robert Stephenson & Hawthorn Ltd
Built:	1951
Works number:	7665
Running number:	No 34
Cylinders:	17in x 16in
Driving Wheels:	2ft 11in
Wheelbase:	5ft 6in
Reservoir pressure:	280psi
Weight:	20ton 5cwt
Length:	18ft 8in
Height:	9ft 4in
At Beckton Gas Works:	1951 – 1971

The first of Beckton's fireless locomotives, designed to work in hazardous areas of potential combustion such as the purifiers. No 7665 was completed on 1st May 1951 and sent to the Gas Works where it became one of the last remaining engines when scrapped on site in 1971 by Dismantling Contractors Ltd of Ewell, Surrey.

NTGB Beckton Gas Works 0-4-0F RSH No 7803

Manufacturer:	Robert Stephenson & Hawthorn Ltd
Built:	1954
Works number:	7803
Running number:	No 35
Cylinders:	17in x 16in
Driving Wheels:	2ft 11in
Wheelbase:	5ft 6in
Reservoir pressure:	280psi
At Beckton Gas Works:	1954 – 1972

The second fireless loco at the Gas Works was RS&H No 7803. Having left the maker's works on 26th July 1954, it remained in use until Beckton's closure. It was then sold in 1972 to Carless, Cape & Leonard Ltd at Harwich Refinery, Parkeston via merchants C & K Metals of Barking. Its final move was to S A Pye at Bramfield, Ipswich in Suffolk on 14th October 2000, where it remains today in a dilapidated state.

GLCC Beckton Gas Works 0-4-0WE Wellman Smith Owen No 5785

Manufacturer:	Wellman Smith Owen Engineering Corporation Ltd
Built:	1953
Works number:	5785
Engine:	80hp
At Beckton Gas Works:	1956 – 1973

The last of three locos put to work at the Beckton coke ovens was completed in 1953 and sent as new to Beckton on 1956. As with its sisters, its time there ended after being taken out of service in 1969 and scrapped in 1973.

Beckton Gas Works first fireless loco was RSH No 7665 which was pictured on 30th October 1954. (J B Latham/ Industrial Locomotive Society)

The second fireless loco to arrive at Beckton was RSH No 7803, which ran as No 35 and survived until sold in 1972. (Author's Collection)

The North Thames Gas Board's first loco purchase was Peckett No 2123, which became Beckton's No 33 and was captured on camera on 12th April 1958. (L R Freeman/ Transport Treasury)

NTGB Beckton Gas Works 4wDM Ruston No 421416

Manufacturer:	Ruston & Hornsby Ltd
Built:	1958
Works number:	421416
Engine:	88DS Ruston 4VPH
Weight:	20ton 0cwt
At Beckton Gas Works:	1958

Experimentation with diesel locos began in earnest in 1958 when Ruston No 421416, new from the maker's works on 20th March that year, was put through it paces at Beckton. It compared less favourably with others from F C Hibberd & Co and was transferred to the small gas works at Lea Bridge where it worked until the railway there was dismantled in 1968. By 1970 it was with the firm of T & M Beaton Brothers at Chiswick before it ended its days at the scrapyard of Keyman, Pearson & Parker Ltd of Walthamstow.

NTGB Beckton Gas Works 4wDM Hibberd No 3885

Manufacturer:	F C Hibberd & Co Ltd
Built:	1958
Works number:	3885
Running number:	No 41
At Beckton Gas Works:	1958 – 1968

First of a pair of locos, the other being No 3889, to appear at Beckton at the beginning of the switch to diesel traction. No 3885 was ex Hibberd's works on 29th September 1958 and remained in service at the gas works until 1968, when the railway system there had been run down, before its sale to W R Cunis Ltd at their Great Coldharbour Rubbish Shoot at Aveley. It worked there until being sold once again to the wharf of Alexander Bruce (Grays) Ltd in 1976. Its final move was to A J Birch & Son Ltd at Hope Farm, Sellinge in Kent by 1986, where it worked until scrapped in February 1991.

NTGB Beckton Gas Works 4wDM Hibberd No 3889

Manufacturer:	F C Hibberd & Co Ltd
Built:	1958
Works number:	3889
Running No:	No 42
At Beckton Gas Works:	1958 – 1968

One of the first pair of new Hibberd diesel locos to arrive at Beckton in 1958, the other being FH No 3885. It remained in service until sold to British Industrial Sand Ltd at Redhill, Surrey in November 1968, where it worked until scrapped in November 1972.

NTGB Beckton Gas Works 4wDM Hibberd No 3907

Manufacturer:	F C Hibberd & Co Ltd
Built:	1959
Works number:	3907
Running No:	No 43
At Beckton Gas Works:	1959 – 1968

The first of six Hibberd locos to arrive at Beckton in 1959 and like several others it was moved on in 1968, in this case to Kensal Green Gas Works in February that year. It worked on there until scrapped in October 1970.

Early days of dieselisation as Hibberd No 3885 draws attention, being only seven months old when pictured on 22nd April 1959. On the right is HE 1335, which survived for only two more months. (Sydney A Leleux)

Hibberd "Planet" loco No 3889 was one of the first pair to arrive at Beckton, where it is seen working as No 42 on 30th April 1960. (R C Riley/Transport Treasury)

NTGB Beckton Gas Works 4wDM Hibberd No 3908

Manufacturer: F C Hibberd & Co Ltd

Built: 1959

Works number: 3908

Running number: No 44

At Beckton Gas Works: 1959 – 1969

The second Hibberd loco to come to Beckton in 1959, FH No 3908 left a little later than others. It was sold to British Industrial Sand Ltd at Redhill, Surrey in February 1969, where it was reunited with FH No 3889. It remained there until being scrapped on site some time between 12th August and 28th December 1986.

NTGB Beckton Gas Works 4wDM Hibberd No 3909

Manufacturer: F C Hibberd & Co Ltd

Built: 1959

Works number: 3909

Running number: No 45

At Beckton Gas Works: 1959 – 1970

The third Hibberd to arrive at Beckton in 1959 was FH No 3909, where it lasted until December 1970 when sold to Wagon Repairs Ltd at Long Eaton in Derbyshire. From there it moved on to the company's other premises at Wellingborough in June 1982, then finally to their works at Stoke on Trent between 21st October 1983 and 20th February 1984. It was eventually scrapped there on 21st June 1993.

NTGB Beckton Gas Works 4wDM Hibberd No 3910

Manufacturer: F C Hibberd & Co Ltd

Built: 1959

Works number: 3910

Running No: No 46

At Beckton Gas Works: 1959 – 1968

The fourth of six Hibberd engines sent to Beckton in 1959 remained in service there until sold to W R Cunis Ltd at the Great Coldharbour Rubbish Shoot at Aveley in 1968. From there it went to British Industrial Sand Ltd at Middleton Towers, Norfolk around February 1975 where it remained until sold for scrap to W Friend Ltd at Watton in March 1982.

FH No 3910 was one of six such locos to arrive at Beckton in 1959. It was photographed there outside the long shed on 20th April 1963. (Alec Swain/Transport Treasury)

NTGB Beckton Gas Works 4wDM Hibberd No 3911

Manufacturer: F C Hibberd & Co Ltd

Built: 1959

Works number: 3911

Running number: No 47

At Beckton Gas Works: 1959 – 1969

The fifth of six Hibberd locos to arrive at Beckton in 1959 was No 3911. It worked there for a decade before being sold in February 1969 to British Industrial Sand Ltd at Middleton Towers in Norfolk, where it was reunited with its former running mate No 3910. It's time there lasted until around May 1977 when it was scrapped on site by W Friend of Watton.

NTGB Beckton Gas Works 4wDM Hibberd No 3912

Manufacturer: F C Hibberd & Co Ltd

Built: 1959

Works number: 3912

Running number: No 48

At Beckton Gas Works: 1959 – 1970

The last of six Hibberd locos that went to Beckton in 1959 was No 3912. This loco remained at the gas works until sold to the Thames Metal Co Ltd at Angerstein's Wharf, Greenwich in September 1970. It was afterwards thought to have been sent for scrap to Pounds Shipbreakers yard in Portsmouth on 31st July 1987.

NTGB Beckton Gas Works 4wDM Hibberd No 3959

Manufacturer: F C Hibberd & Co Ltd

Built: 1961

Works number: 3959

Running No: No 49

At Beckton Gas Works: 1961 – 1970

The first of the final batch of three Hibberd locos delivered to Beckton in 1961, this loco remained at the gas works until June 1970 when it was sold to Edward Ash (Plant) Ltd at Deptford. From there it went via dealer T W Ward Ltd to the Powell Duffryn Wagon Co Ltd at Maindy Works Glamorgan in January 1972, where it worked until a further move took it to the company's Haywood Works in Greater Manchester some time between 11th October 1990 and 18th April 1991. It was last reported there when the works closed on 6th February 1993 and is presumed scrapped around that time.

NTGB Beckton Gas Works 4wDM Hibberd No 3960

Manufacturer: F C Hibberd & Co Ltd

Built: 1961

Works number: 3960

Running No: No 50

At Beckton Gas Works: 1961 – 1970

The second of three Hibberd locos delivered to Beckton in 1961, FH No 3960 worked there until December 1970 when it was sold to Wagon Repairs Ltd at Stoke-on-Trent, Staffordshire. It was afterwards noted as out-of-use there in 1984 and scrapped in November that year.

NTGB Beckton Gas Works 4wDM Hibberd No 3961

Manufacturer: F C Hibberd & Co Ltd

Built: 1961

Works number: 3961

Running number: No 51

At Beckton Gas Works: 1961 – 1971

The last of a trio of Hibberd locos delivered in 1961, FH No 3961 was the final locomotive ordered by the North Thames Gas Board and attained the highest running number of No 51 at the Gas Works. In 1971 it was sold to C & K Metals Ltd at Barking where it remained until November 1972 when it joined Nos 3889 and 3908 at British Industrial Sand Ltd at Redhill, Surrey. From there it moved to Resco Railways at Woolwich some time between 3rd March and 6th May 1979 before being exported to Henry Boot in Hong Kong on 20th September 1980.

Locomotives Purchased by North Thames Gas Board at Beckton Gas Works						
Maker	**Works No**	**Date Built**	**Type**	**Running No**	**Date Arrived**	**Date Departed**
S	9398	1950	0-4-0VBT	n/a	1951	1951
P	2123	1951	0-4-0ST	33	1951	1962
RSH	7665	1951	0-4-0F	34	1951	1971
RSH	7803	1954	0-4-0F	35	1954	1972
WSO	5785	1953	0-4-0WE	n/a	1956	1973
RH	421416	1958	4wDM	n/a	1958	1958
FH	3885	1958	4wDM	41	1958	1968
FH	3889	1958	4wDM	42	1958	1968
FH	3907	1959	4wDM	43	1959	1968
FH	3908	1959	4wDM	44	1959	1969
FH	3909	1959	4wDM	45	1959	1970
FH	3910	1959	4wDM	46	1959	1968
FH	3911	1959	4wDM	47	1959	1969
FH	3912	1959	4wDM	48	1959	1970
FH	3959	1961	4wDM	49	1961	1970
FH	3960	1961	4wDM	50	1961	1970
FH	3961	1961	4wDM	51	1961	1971
Note: S No 9398 on trial – returned to maker						

CHAPTER 5

The Beckton Branch Line 1872-1971

The ground level railway at the gas works had evolved at the same time as the overhead system . To connect it to the outside world, the Gas Light & Coke Company built a branch line, which joined the North Woolwich Railway a mile to the east of Custom House and ran for almost two miles. Along its route, the branch line crossed East Ham Manor Way, where there was a level crossing and signal box, before passing what is now Winsor Terrace and terminating at a new station named "Beckton".

At Beckton, a single platform stood to the north of a marshalling yard with five sidings. Along with the seldom-used booking office, the platform was completed with a waiting shelter and a signal box. From the outset the line was leased to, and operated by, the Great Eastern Railway. There was also, at one time, an internal station inside the works named "Beckton Gasworks" which had existed in the 1890s but was gone by 1904.

Initially, freight trains ran on the line from 14th October 1872, along with some workman's trains, until a public service was opened on 18th March 1874. At its peak there were seven passenger trains each way on Monday to Saturday, and just one on Sundays, while Beckton station was generally unstaffed with tickets being issued and collected at Custom House.

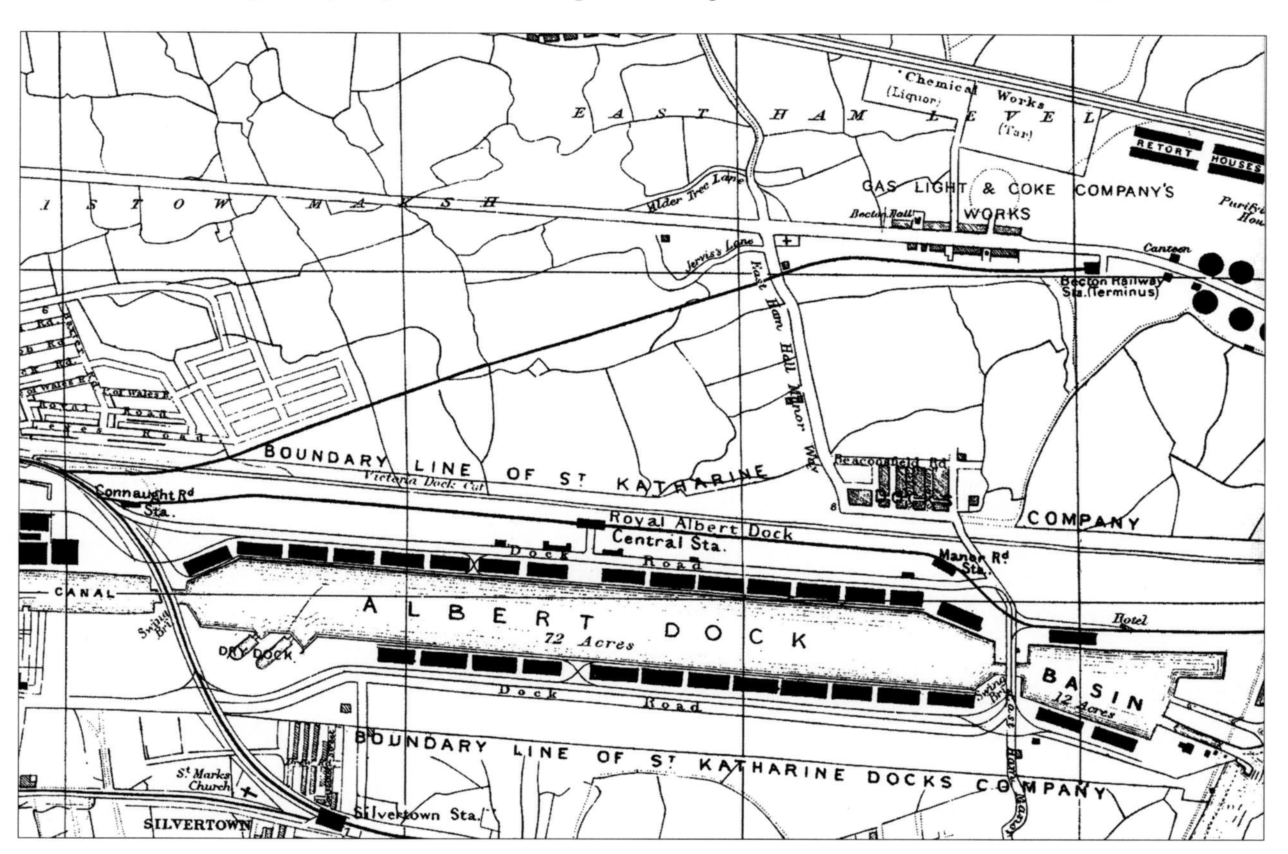

An 1888 map showing the route of the Beckton Branch and its junction with the North Woolwich Line. (Author's Collection)

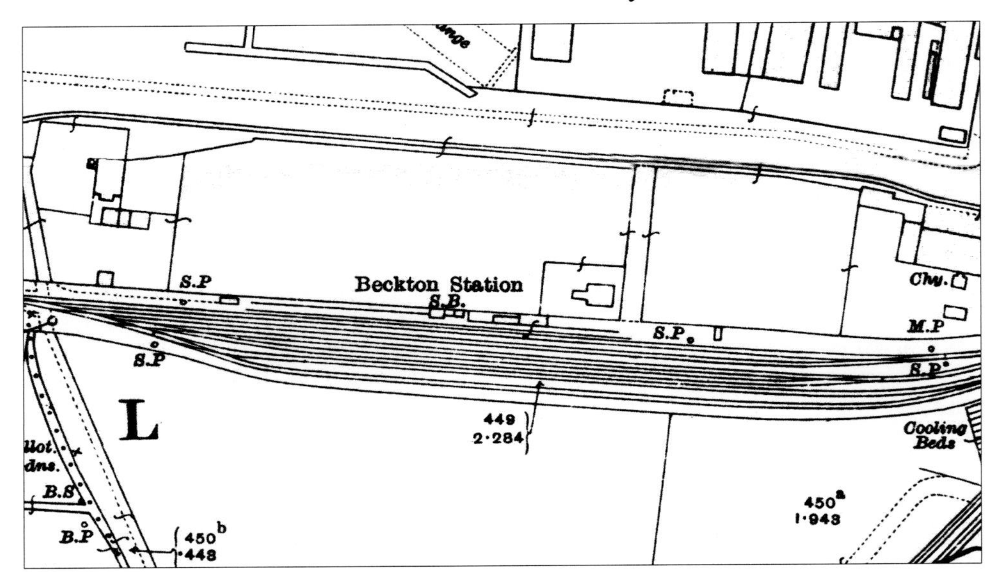

Beckton Station was the branch line terminus on the doorstep of the works, shown in this map of 1914. (Crown Copyright)

A dismal Beckton Station looms from the damp and mist in the 1930s. LNER class J15 No 7898 steams beside the assorted wagons on the exchange sidings. (Peter Smith Collection)

Another view of the exchange sidings alongside Beckton Station, with the LNER class J15 about to depart. (Peter Smith Collection)

Looking eastwards at Beckton station in the 1930s as a solitary traveller awaits his train. (Disused Stations Collection)

The line later suffered competition, first from the local tram network, and then from a new bus service initiated in 1927. After severe damage by enemy bombing in September 1940 it was repaired by the then operators LNER and reopened, but its reprieve was brief as it closed to passengers on 29th December that year. Freight trains continued to operate, especially during the war years when most coal arrived by rail instead of from ships due to the threat to vessels in the North Sea and bombing of the exposed riverside jetties. Remnants of the station remained into the 1960s but now all traces are gone, the site having been redeveloped. The final train from Beckton ran through the gas works on its way out from the Products Factory on 1st June 1970, and the branch to Custom House officially closed in February 1971, following which, the tracks had been lifted within two years.

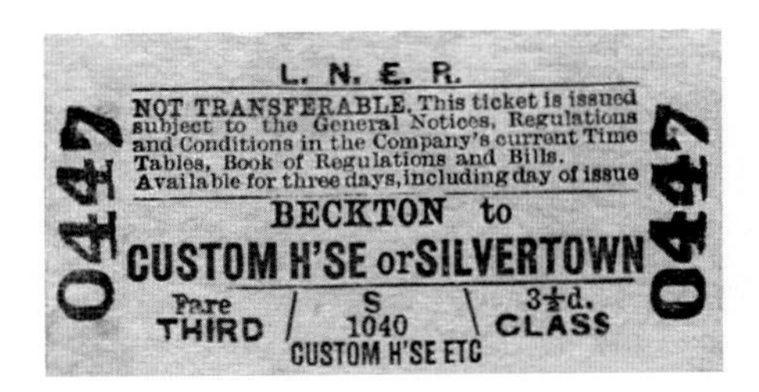

A busy Beckton station, but things are not as they seem. This photo was dated 1958 but Beckton had closed to passengers in 1940. It is thought these are members of a party touring the gas works railway system taking time to study the obsolete platform. (John Mann Collection/Disused Stations)

The remains of Beckton Station, long after it ceased to function, showing the signal box, passenger shelter and booking office. (Peter Smith Collection)

Looking north across the Manor Way level crossing in 1928 towards the church of St Michael and all Angels. Manhole maintenance is resumed after the passing tram moves off towards East Ham. The tram system had taken much of the passenger trade from the branch line by this time. (Courtesy of Newham Heritage and Archives)

The level crossing with its dilapidated signal box and gates at East Ham Manor Way looking towards Beckton on 2nd December 1967. The signal box was a replacement following wartime bombing in 1940. (Ian Baker)

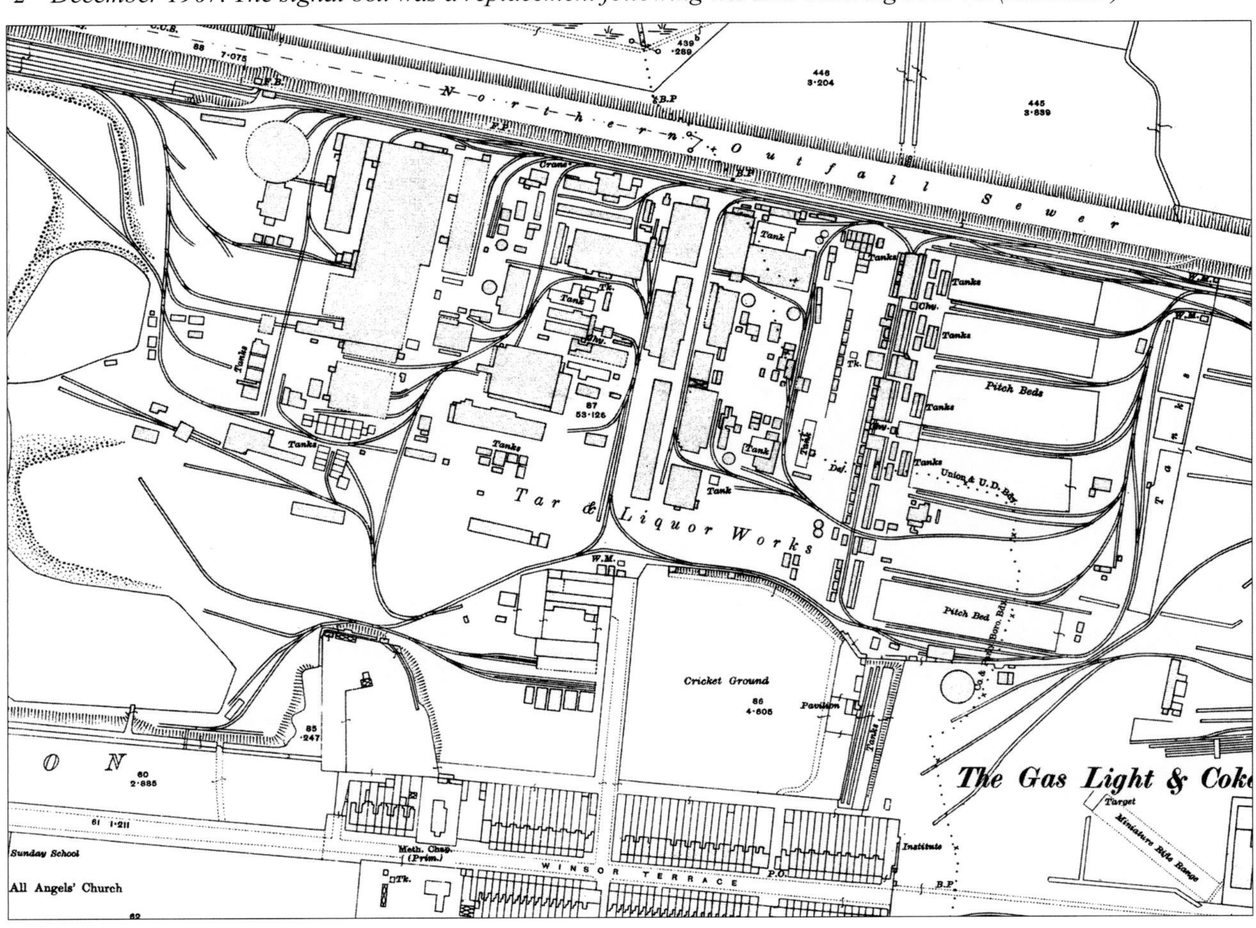

CHAPTER 6

Beckton Products Works
The Gas Light & Coke Company 1879-1949

The GLCC's various gas works produced a mixture of by-products, such as oils, resin and tar, that were then sold off at nominal rates. However, the output from Beckton was so great it raised commercial opportunities to process them "in house" as viable market commodities. The GLCC set up an additional factory to the north west of the gas works in 1879. At first this was deemed part of the main works and managed by them but by 1882 it had become a stand-alone business with its own administration and, with its output of tar, pitch, creosote and acids, was soon creating a healthy share of the GLCC profits. In its early days, the plant was referred to as the "Tar and Liquor Works" but over the years its output included many petrochemical products such as benzene and ammonia.

Initially, locos from the Gas Works were used around the Products factory system but, in keeping with its later independence from the Gas Works, from 1892 the Products Works purchased its own locomotives, with the first four arriving that year. As with the Gas Works, these were all obtained from Neilson & Co as Nos 4444, 4445, 4571 and 4572, with running Nos 1–4. It was 1898 before the next loco appeared, but this was from Neilson Reid & Co, successors to Neilson & Co from that year. This was No 5348, followed by NR 6302 in 1902. As with the main GLCC works, no further dealings with the Neilson Company were made after 1902 following appearance the two self built locos at the gas works, and all subsequent purchases were from other manufacturers.

Above: *An early view of the Products Works showing one of the Gas Works engines with a sulphate train in 1881. The Products Division did not have its own locos until 1892. (Courtesy of Newham Heritage and Archives)*

Opposite page: *The Gas Light & Coke Company's By-Products Works showing the railway system in 1914. The line connecting to the Gas Works system is at the top right on the south side of the outfall sewer. The Company houses along Winsor Terrace can be seen at the bottom of the map. (Crown Copyright)*

Although the Products Works railway was independent of the Gas Works, the two were connected and locomotives from each stable often met when Products engines ran trains through the Gas Works to the exchange sidings at Beckton Station. Rail duties at the Products Works were not as arduous as at the Gas Works where locos worked round the clock to feed and service the insatiable retorts, and a fleet of 15 engines was sufficient to shunt and marshal the output from the factory. The works had its own loco shed that could house ten engines. In early years, loco repairs were carried out in the Gas Works maintenance workshops but later, the Product Works built its own railway maintenance shops in 1952. As mentioned previously, the Products locos had their own distinct maroon livery and carried running numbers on their smokebox doors. They also operated the rope runner system of the Gas Works, whereby the fireman performed the uncoupling of wagons by way of ropes to the front and rear of the engine.

The next loco to arrive was Andrew Barclay, No 757 of 1898 vintage, which came to Beckton Products Works in 1916. This had previously been a contractor's engine and the purchase of a second hand loco was probably due to shortages caused by the war.

Barclay No 757 survived only until being sold sometime around 1920 and was replaced by another from the same maker, this time an older loco, No 730 built 1893, which was also second hand and appeared in 1921. Running as No 8 it arrived a little out of sequence after having been rebuilt by John F Wake & Co Ltd.

The first engine purchased new after WWI was Peckett No 1576, which also came in 1921 but a return to the second-hand market came in 1946 when Hawthorn Leslie No 3308 came from a plastics factory in Staffordshire. This was followed by another of the same maker when fireless engine HL No 3595 came from nearby Barking Power Station. Two new Peckett locos, Nos 2083 and 2089 arrived in 1947 and 1948 respectively. And these were the final purchases by the Products Works in the GLCC era, after which the North Thames Gas Board took control.

Above: *As with the Gas Works, the Products Works had its own fleet of internal wagons. These two, pictured on 15th March 1961 were for the disposal of clinker. (Sydney A Leleux)*
Opposite page: *Diagram of the Beckton Product Works in 1938, showing the railway system and main buildings. (Map by Roger Hateley)*

Peckett No 2083 (No 14) heads a train of GLCC tanker wagons at the Products Works. Each has a capacity of 13 tons and bears the inscription "Empty to the Tar & Ammonia Works, Beckton, LNER". (Courtesy of Newham Heritage and Archives)

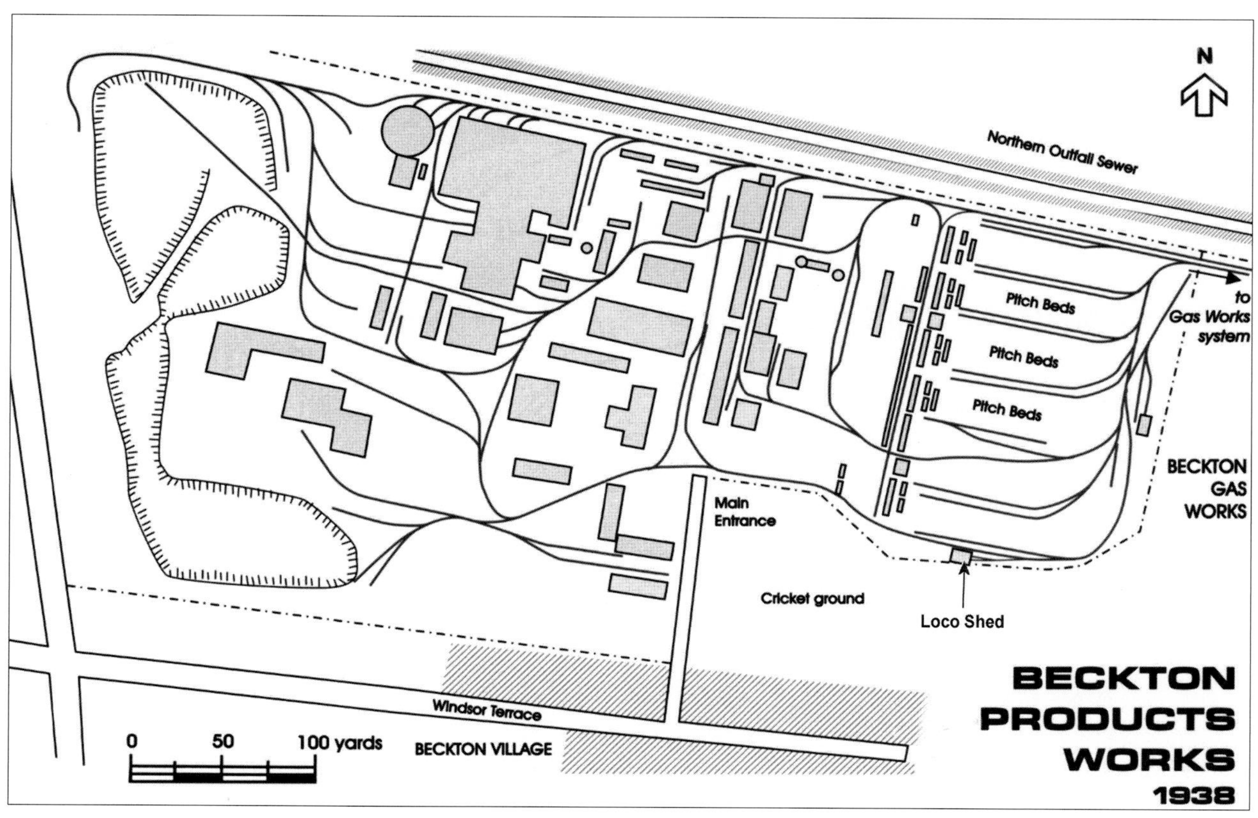

GLCC Beckton Products Works 0-4-0T Neilson No 4444

Manufacturer:	Neilson & Co Ltd
Built:	1892
Works number:	4444
Running number:	No 1
Cylinders:	12in x 20in
Driving Wheels:	3ft 0in
Wheelbase:	5ft 0in
Boiler pressure:	160psi
Weight:	19ton 10cwt
At Beckton Products Works:	1892 – 1968

The initial locomotives for the Products Works were ordered from Neilson & Co who were the main suppliers of engines to the Gas Works. Four arrived from that maker in 1892, the first being No 4444 which ran as the works No 1. After leading a long and successful life there it became the sole survivor of the Products locos when preserved at Bressingham Steam Museum at Diss, Norfolk in October 1968.

GLCC Beckton Products Works 0-4-0T Neilson No 4445

Manufacturer:	Neilson & Co Ltd
Built:	1892
Works number:	4445
Running number:	No 2
Cylinders:	12in x 20in
Driving Wheels:	3ft 0in
Wheelbase:	5ft 0in
Boiler pressure:	120psi
Weight:	19ton 10cwt
At Beckton Products Works:	1892 – 1967

Like No 4444, this was one of the heavier Neilson designs at the Products Works. It was one of the longer serving locos there when scrapped around July 1967.

GLCC Beckton Products Works 0-4-0T Neilson No 4571

Manufacturer:	Neilson & Co Ltd
Built:	1892
Works number:	4571
Running number:	No 3
Cylinders:	10in x 18in
Driving Wheels:	2ft 10in
Wheelbase:	5ft 0in
Boiler pressure:	160psi
Weight:	16ton 10cwt
At Beckton Products Works:	1892 – 1966

No 4571 was one of the smaller Neilsons that were standard design at Beckton Gas Works. In fact, after working most of its life at the Products Works it was transferred to join others of its type at the Gas Works in 1966 where it lasted another two years before being broken up in 1968.

The Products Works No 1 loco was Neilson No 4444, which became its only survivor when taken into preservation. (Douglas Clayton Collection/ Industrial Railway Society)

The second Neilson at the Products Works in 1892 was No 4445, seen here running as the No 2 engine on 12th April 1958. (L R Freeman/ Transport Treasury)

The third Neilson at Beckton Products was No 4571, pictured standing on the siding near the loco shed on 24th August 1957. (R C Riley/Transport Treasury)

GLCC Beckton Products Works 0-4-0T Neilson No 4572

Manufacturer:	Neilson & Co Ltd
Built:	1892
Works number:	4572
Running number:	No 4
Cylinders:	10in x 18in
Driving Wheels:	2ft 10in
Wheelbase:	5ft 0in
Boiler pressure:	120psi
Weight:	16ton 10cwt
At Beckton Products Works:	1892 – 1961

Neilson No 4571 was the last of a quartet delivered to the Products Works in 1892. Having been rebuilt at Beckton in 1930 it was also the first of the four to be disposed of when scrapped on site by Thomas W Ward Ltd in June 1961.

GLCC Beckton Products Works 0-4-0T Neilson Reid No 5348

Manufacturer:	Neilson Reid & Co Ltd
Built:	1898
Works number:	5348
Running number:	No 5
Cylinders:	10in x 18in
Driving Wheels:	2ft 10in
Wheelbase:	5ft 0in
Boiler pressure:	120psi
Weight:	16ton 10cwt
At Beckton Products Works:	1898 – 1961

Neilson & Co Ltd became Neilson Reid & Co Ltd in 1898 and continued producing the same designs in a continuation of the works number series. One of their first locos was No 5348, the first of two that were acquired by the Products Works. It was rebuilt in 1925 at Beckton and its days there ended when broken up on site by Thomas W Ward Ltd in June 1961.

GLCC Beckton Products Works 0-4-0T Neilson Reid No 6302

Manufacturer:	Neilson Reid & Co Ltd
Built:	1902
Works number:	6302
Running number:	No 6
Cylinders:	10in x 18in
Driving Wheels:	2ft 10in
Wheelbase:	5ft 0in
Boiler pressure:	160psi
Weight:	16ton 10cwt
At Beckton Products Works:	1902 – 1961

This was the last Neilson loco supplied to Beckton before relations were strained over the "in house" building of two similarly designed engines by the GLCC at the Gas Works. As No 6 it worked on until withdrawn in 1957 and was gradually dismantled for spares, the remainder of the loco was broken up on site by H F A Dolman Ltd of Southend in January 1961.

A rare photo of AB No 757 pictured in its later days at Trent Concrete Ltd in Nottingham. (Frank Jones Collection/ Industrial Locomotive Society)

The first of several Peckett locos supplied to the Products Works was No 1574 where it was pictured as their No 9 engine. (Douglas Clayton Collection/Industrial Railway Society)

GLCC Beckton Products Works 0-4-0ST Peckett No 1575

Manufacturer:	Peckett & Sons Ltd
Built:	1920
Works number:	1575
Running number:	No 10
Cylinders:	10in x 16in
Driving Wheels:	2ft 7in
Wheelbase:	5ft 0in
Boiler pressure:	160psi
Weight:	17ton 15cwt
Height:	8ft 9in
At Beckton Products Works:	1920 – 1962

A second Peckett for the Products Works was completed a month later than No 1574, in December 1920, and became No 10 at Beckton. Unfortunately, its time there was less than its sister as it was scrapped in July 1962.

The Products Works second Peckett loco was No 1575 supplied as No 10 in 1920. In the background is NR No 5348. (Douglas Clayton Collection/Industrial Railway Society)

GLCC Beckton Products Works 0-4-0ST Barclay No 730

Manufacturer:	Andrew Barclay, Sons & Co Ltd
Built:	1893
Works number:	730
Running number:	No 8
Cylinders:	10in x 18in
Driving Wheels:	3ft 0in
Wheelbase:	5ft 0in
Boiler pressure:	160psi
Weight:	17ton 10cwt
At Beckton Products Works:	1921 – 1961

Like the Products Works other Barclay (No 757) this loco was also a former contractor's engine, having been supplied to Robert McAlpine & Sons Ltd on 18th April 1893. After use on the construction of Dunston Power Station it was sold to candle makers Mawson Clark & Co Ltd at their Dunston Works in Durham around 1910. From there it was in the hands of dealers J F Wake of Darlington in 1916 until being sold on to the Products Works, arriving there in 1921. Its working life at Beckton was relatively short at 40 years when scrapped on site, along with three other locos, by Thomas W Ward Ltd in June 1961.

Barclay No 730 had something of a history before becoming the Products Works No 8 engine. (Industrial Railway Society Collection)

GLCC Beckton Products Works 0-4-0ST Peckett No 1576

Manufacturer:	Peckett & Sons Ltd
Built:	1921
Works number:	1576
Running number:	No 11
Cylinders:	12in x 18in
Driving Wheels:	2ft 11in
Wheelbase:	5ft 6in
Boiler pressure:	160psi
Weight:	22ton 10cwt
Height:	9ft 3in
At Beckton Products Works:	1921 – 1961

The third Peckett to arrive at Beckton's Products Works was No 1576. This was a special version of the maker's R2 class and was completed in January 1921. It was bigger and more powerful than the previous two, but its time there ended when scrapped on site by Thomas W Ward Ltd in June 1961.

GLCC Beckton Products Works 0-4-0ST Hawthorn, Leslie No 3308

Manufacturer:	R & W Hawthorn, Leslie & Co Ltd
Built:	1918
Works number:	3308
Running number:	No 13
Cylinders:	12in x 18in
Driving Wheels:	3ft 0in
Wheelbase:	5ft 6in
Boiler pressure:	160psi
Weight:	21ton 15cwt
At Beckton Products Works:	1946 – 1967

Hawthorn, Leslie No 3308 came to Beckton in July 1946, having previously worked at the firm of British Industrial Plastics Ltd, Oldbury in Staffordshire, where it had been purchased new in 1918. After a couple of decades of service at the Products Works, it became one of several Beckton locos scrapped in July 1967.

GLCC Beckton Products Works 0-4-0F Hawthorn, Leslie No 3595

Manufacturer:	R & W Hawthorn, Leslie & Co Ltd
Built:	1924
Works number:	3595
Running number:	No 12
Cylinders:	17in x 16in
Driving Wheels:	2ft 11in
Wheelbase:	5ft 6in
Boiler pressure:	160psi
Weight:	18ton 10cwt
At Beckton Products Works:	1947 – 1969

The second Hawthorn, Leslie loco No 3595 was distinctive for two reasons. Firstly, it was a fireless engine, purchased especially to work in hazardous areas such as the benzole plant. Secondly, it was the only Products Works loco to sport a cab. Having been completed at the makers on 19th August 1924, it had been delivered new to the nearby County of London Electric Supply Co Ltd at Barking Power Station, where it worked until around March 1947 before moving to Beckton. It remained there until 1969, after which its fate is unknown.

The third Peckett delivered to the Products Works was heavier then the previous two arrivals and is pictured there at the water tower by the running shed entrance. (Douglas Clayton Collection/Industrial Railway Society)

The yard at the Products Works where Hawthorn, Leslie No 3308 is in tandem with Neilson No 4444 on 15th March 1961. (Sydney A Leleux)

The Products Works only Fireless loco was HL No 3595 seen on duty there on 2nd September 1964. (Roger Hateley)

GLCC Beckton Products Works 0-4-0ST Peckett No 2083

Manufacturer:	Peckett & Sons Ltd
Built:	1947
Works number:	2083
Running number:	No 14
Cylinders:	12in x 20in
Driving Wheels:	3ft 0in
Wheelbase:	5ft 3in
Boiler pressure:	180psi
Weight:	23ton 0cwt
At Beckton Products Works:	1947 – 1967

One of a final pair of Peckett locos that were the last engines to be purchased at the Products Works. No 2083 was ex maker's works on 14th July 1947, being a special adaptation of the R4 class. Its time at Beckton lasted exactly twenty years when, along with several others, it was scrapped in July 1967.

GLCC Beckton Products Works 0-4-0ST Peckett No 2099

Manufacturer:	Peckett & Sons Ltd
Built:	1948
Works number:	2099
Running number:	No 15
Cylinders:	12in x 20in
Driving Wheels:	3ft 0in
Wheelbase:	5ft 3in
Boiler pressure:	180psi
Weight:	23ton 0cwt
At Beckton Products Works:	1948 – 1962

This final acquisition by the Products Works was completed by the makers on 31st August 1948 and its arrival at Beckton marked the end of locomotive purchases there. Like its sister No 2083 it was a scaled down version of Peckett's R4 class but its career lasted only fourteen years as it was scrapped in July 1962. An incredibly short life for a steam locomotive.

The first of two Peckett locos supplied in the post WWII years. No 2083 was one of a pair of that were the final engines purchased new at the Products Works. It was photographed there on 24th August 1957. (R C Riley/ Transport Treasury)

The Products Works final locomotive was Peckett No 2099 but its time there was short lived when it was scrapped after just fourteen years service. (Douglas Clayton Collection/Industrial Railway Society)

Summary of all locos purchased by GLCC for the Products Works						
Maker	**Works No**	**Date Built**	**Type**	**Running No**	**Date Arrived**	**Date Departed**
N	4444	1892	0-4-0T	1	1892	1968
N	4445	1892	0-4-0T	2	1892	1967
N	4571	1892	0-4-0T	3	1892	1966
N	4572	1892	0-4-0T	4	1892	1961
NR	5348	1898	0-4-0T	5	1898	1961
NR	6302	1902	0-4-0T	6	1902	1961*
AB	757	1895	0-4-0ST	7	1916	1920
P	1574	1920	0-4-0ST	9	1920	1967
P	1575	1920	0-4-0ST	10	1920	1962
AB	730	1893	0-4-0ST	8	1921	1961
P	1576	1921	0-4-0ST	11	1921	1961
HL	3308	1918	0-4-0ST	13	1946	1967
HL	3595	1924	0-4-0F	12	1947	1969
P	2083	1947	0-4-0ST	14	1947	1967
P	2099	1948	0-4-0ST	15	1948	1962
* Out of use from 1957 but used for spares						

Summary of locos acquired by North Thames Gas Board at the Products Works in 1949						
Maker	**Works No**	**Date Built**	**Type**	**Running No**	**Date Arrived**	**Date Departed**
N	4444	1892	0-4-0T	1	1892	1968
N	4445	1892	0-4-0T	2	1892	1967
N	4571	1892	0-4-0T	3	1892	1966
N	4572	1892	0-4-0T	4	1892	1961
NR	5348	1898	0-4-0T	5	1898	1961
NR	6302	1902	0-4-0T	6	1902	1957
P	1574	1920	0-4-0ST	9	1920	1967
P	1575	1920	0-4-0ST	10	1920	1962
AB	730	1893	0-4-0ST	8	1921	1961
P	1576	1921	0-4-0ST	11	1921	1961
HL	3308	1918	0-4-0ST	13	1946	1967
HL	3595	1924	0-4-0F	12	1947	1969
P	2083	1947	0-4-0ST	14	1947	1967
P	2099	1948	0-4-0ST	15	1948	1962

CHAPTER 7

Beckton Products Works

The North Thames Gas Board 1949-1970

Following the nationalisation of the gas industry, the Products Works also came under the new regime, and all but one of the of the GLCC locos (No 7 – AB No 757 had been sold) were taken over by the Gas Board who, after realising the huge potential of the factory, invested heavily over the next decade. In providing new facilities, extending and modernising production lines and building more processing plants, it became one of the largest such industries in the world. In addition, the numerous small workshops around the works were updated and new mechanical workshops, with a floor space of 80,000 square feet, were opened by the chairman of the Gas Council on 2nd October 1952. This was fully equipped with stores and offices, together with overhead travelling cranes and facilities to service and rebuild locomotives and rolling stock.

However, all was not well, as from 1954 the cost of British coal had risen by 40% and the NTGB was forced to buy stocks from overseas. Despite this, the manufacture of chemicals at the Products Works rose steadily and reached a peak in 1957. But by the 1960s, with natural gas coming ashore from the North Sea oilfields, the production of coal gas was nearing its end. This saw a dramatic decline in output at the Gas Works, while the Products Works, being almost totally dependant on its neighbour, was equally devastated. Reduced activity at both facilities and decreasing demand on their railway operations saw something of an amalgamation of resources from the two loco fleets and several engines found themselves working on each other's territories.

The workshop facilities at the Products Works were greatly improved from 1952. Here, Neilson No 4572 awaits repair on 24th August 1957. (R M Casserley)

More activity at the Product Works workshops where HL No 3308 awaits attention between other locos on 12th April 1958. (L S Freeman/Transport Treasury)

Looking down on the Products Works shed yard on 18th June 1955. On view are HL No 3308 nearest the camera with (L-R) N 4445, P 2099 and N 4572. (Philip J Kelley)

Busy times at the Products Works loco shed yard on 12th April 1958 where P No 2083 (left) stands in line with P No 2099, N No 4445 and P No 1576. On the right is P No 1575 with HL No 3595 ahead of it. (L S Freeman/Transport Treasury)

Another view on 12th April 1958 where Peckett No 1575 simmers outside the loco shed ahead of Neilson No 4444. (L S Freeman/ Transport Treasury)

Nielsen Reid No 6302 had been condemned and dismantled for spares in 1957 with its remains finally taken away in 1961. This was a year when Neilson No 4572, and Neilson Reid No 5348 were disposed of along with Barclay No 730 and Peckett No 1576, which were both broken up on site in June. The end for two more Pecketts came when Nos 1575 and 2099 were sold for scrap in 1962.

The final scrappings came in 1967 when Neilson No 4445, Peckett Nos 1574 and 2083, along with HL 3308 were done away with. In those final years, as rail demand lessened and the degree of maintenance was relaxed, the Products Works locos looked considerably worse for wear. The remaining two locos were saved from the cutter's torch with Neilson No 4444, the Products Works No 1 engine, being preserved at Bressingham Steam Museum in 1968 and the fireless HL No 3595 being sold in 1969.

At the Gas Works, production of coal gas had ceased in June 1969 and activity the Product Works was wound down with plant being dismantled soon afterwards. At the very end, the Products Works had the distinction of sending the last train out from Beckton when a cargo of pitch was hauled away at 5.15 pm on 1st July 1970. The internal rail system was then ripped up, thus ending a unique chapter of industrial railway history that had lasted for a century.

Quite remarkably, apart from the preserved locomotives, almost nothing remains of the huge railway system that covered both the Gas Works and Products Works. Two signal arms (each owned by separate individuals) and a solitary internal wagon, now residing at the Buckinghamshire Railway Centre, are all that is left.

The Products Works No 15 (Peckett No 2099) looking slightly dilapidated when shunting on 15th March 1961. (Sydney A Leleux)

Hawthorn, Leslie No 3308 was a comparative latecomer to Beckton, arriving second hand in 1946. It was photographed at the Products Works on 2nd September 1964. (Roger Hateley)

The condemned line at the Products works on 15th March 1961 where Neilson No 4572 (centre) and Neilson Reid No 5348 (behind) await their fate. (Sydney A Leleux)

Summary of all locos purchased by GLCC and NTGB for the Gas Works and Products Works						
Maker	**Works No**	**Date Built**	**Type**	**Running No**	**Date Arrived**	**Date Departed**
			Gas Works			
N	1561	1870	0-4-0WT	1	1870	1963
N	1562	1870	0-4-0WT	2	1870	1938
N	1659	1872	0-4-0WT	3	1872	1934
Chaplin	1675	1874	0-4-0VBT	1	1874	c1900
Chaplin	1756	1874	0-4-0VBT	2	1874	c1900
Chaplin	1757	1874	0-4-0VBT	3	1874	c1900
MW	457	1875	0-4-0ST	4	1875	1931
N	2151	1876	0-4-0WT	5	1876	1927
N	2227	1877	0-4-0WT	6	1877	1934
N	2228	1877	0-4-0WT	7	1877	1934
N	2380	1878	0-4-0WT	8	1878	1934
N	2382	1878	0-4-0T	9	1878	1938
N	2465	1879	0-4-0T	10	1879	1962
N	2466	1879	0-4-0T	11	1879	1961
N	2597	1880	0-4-0T	12	1880	1960
N	2598	1880	0-4-0T	13	1880	1967
N	3097	1883	0-4-0ST	14	1883	1935
N	3345	1884	0-4-0ST	15	1884	1930
N	3451	1885	0-4-0ST	16	1885	1958
BH	865	1886	0-4-0ST	17	1886	1958
BH	864	1886	0-4-0T	18	1886	1959
N	3789	1888	0-4-0T	19	1888	1962
N	4249	1890	0-4-0T	20	1890	1960
N	4250	1890	0-4-0ST	21	1890	1959
N	4414	1891	0-4-0T	22	1891	1960
N	4408	1892	0-4-0T	23	1892	1967
N	5086	1896	0-4-0T	24	1896	1958
N	5087	1896	0-4-0ST	25	1896	1961
N	5228	1897	0-4-0T	26	1897	1960
N	5229	1897	0-4-0T	27	1897	1962
N	5230	1897	0-4-0T	28	1897	1962
N	5231	1897	0-4-0T	29	1897	1962
Beckton	1	1902	0-4-0T	30	1902	1960

The North Thames Gas Board 1949-1970

Maker	Works No	Date Built	Type	Running No	Date Arrived	Date Departed
Beckton	2	1902	0-4-0T	31	1902	1959
MW	901	1885	0-4-0ST	32	1909	1912
MW	1832	1913	0-4-0ST	32	1913	1955
AB	636	1889	0-4-0ST	33	1916	1949
AB	262	1883	0-4-0ST	34	1916	1935
AB	957	1902	0-4-0ST	35	1917	1949
AB	266	1884	0-4-0ST	36	1917	1918
HC	657	1903	0-4-0ST	38	1918	1938
AB	?	?	0-4-0ST	39	1918	1920
HC	287	1887	0-4-0ST	37	1919	1930
HE	1335	1919	0-4-0ST	40	1919	1959
BgC	790	1920	2w-2PMR	n/a	1920	1930s
AB	1720	1921	0-4-0T	41 (4)	1921	1961
AB	1721	1921	0-4-0T	42 (36)	1921	1961
AB	1722	1921	0-4-0T	43 (39)	1921	1960
BgC	1335	1923	2w-2PMR	n/a	1923	1930s
S	6951	1927	0-4-0VBT	2	1927	1938
HL	3742	1929	0-4-0ST	5	1929	1932
WSO	1408	1929	0-4-0WE	n/a	1929	1973
P	1811	1930	0-4-0ST	15	1930	1959
HL	3794	1931	0-4-0ST	5	1931	1959
P	1837	1931	0-4-0ST	37	1931	1962
AW	D23	1933	0-4-0DE	n/a	1934	1934
P	1932	1937	0-4-0ST	3	1937	1959
P	1933	1937	0-4-0ST	6	1937	1960
P	1966	1939	0-4-0ST	2	1939	1967
WB	2657	1942	0-4-0ST	7	1942	1967
WB	2658	1942	0-4-0ST	8	1942	1961
WSO	4191	1945	0-4-0WE	n/a	1945	1973
MW	1427	1899	0-4-0ST	9	1946	1959
HC	522	1899	0-4-0ST	38	1947	1958
RSH	7474	1949	0-4-0ST	14	1949	1962
P	2123	1951	0-4-0ST	33	1951	1962
RSH	7665	1951	0-4-0F	34	1951	1971
S	9398	1950	0-4-0VBT	n/a	1951	1951

Beckton's Railways and Locomotives

Maker	Works No	Date Built	Type	Running No	Date Arrived	Date Departed
WSO	5785	1953	0-4-0WE	n/a	1953	1973
RSH	7803	1954	0-4-0F	35	1954	1972
FH	3885	1958	4wDM	41	1958	1968
FH	3889	1958	4wDM	42	1958	1968
RH	421416	1958	4wDM	n/a	1958	1958
FH	3907	1959	4wDM	43	1959	1968
FH	3908	1959	4wDM	44	1959	1969
FH	3909	1959	4wDM	45	1959	1970
FH	3910	1959	4wDM	46	1959	1968
FH	3911	1959	4wDM	47	1959	1969
FH	3912	1959	4wDM	48	1959	1970
FH	3959	1961	4wDM	49	1961	1970
FH	3960	1961	4wDM	50	1961	1970
FH	3961	1961	4wDM	51	1961	1971
Products Works						
N	4444	1892	0-4-0T	1	1892	1968
N	4445	1892	0-4-0T	2	1892	1967
N	4571	1892	0-4-0T	3	1892	1966
N	4572	1892	0-4-0T	4	1892	1961
NR	5348	1898	0-4-0T	5	1898	1961
NR	6302	1902	0-4-0T	6	1902	1957
AB	757	1895	0-4-0ST	7	1916	1920
P	1574	1920	0-4-0ST	9	1920	1967
P	1575	1920	0-4-0ST	10	1920	1962
AB	730	1893	0-4-0ST	8	1921	1961
P	1576	1921	0-4-0ST	11	1921	1961
HL	3308	1918	0-4-0ST	13	1946	1967
HL	3595	1924	0-4-0F	12	1947	1969
P	2083	1947	0-4-0ST	14	1947	1967
P	2099	1948	0-4-0ST	15	1948	1962

CHAPTER 8

Beckton Outfall Works Contractors 1861-1957

Although the railways at Beckton's Gas Works dominated the scene, there was also a smaller and lesser-known system on its doorstep, that of the city's Northern Outfall and Sewage Works. In fact, this neighbouring line had its beginnings a decade before that of the Gas Works. The outfall and its treatment works were home to several railways over more than a century and, in total, saw a large number of locomotives come and go in its time. The Sewage Works itself operated five locos but those of various contractors, during building and improvement works, swelled the total to at least 28 from 1861 to 1964.

Until relatively modern times, before improvements to roads and heavy machinery, contractors engaged in large constructions used their own railway systems to receive materials and move heavy loads around sites. Many of these builders had a stable of locomotives that were moved around the various works. Some were bought especially for each contract, then written of as scrap or sold to other firms. Though not strictly a contractor, London County Council carried out many of its works programmes "in house" rather than outsourcing and, in doing so, acquired several locomotives of their own.

George Furness – Northern Outfall Sewer 1861–1865

With the city's population rapidly expanding in the mid 1800s, the problem of sewage disposal had become acute. While it was being dumped untreated, directly into the Thames, the stench from pollution and its effect on drinking water required radical action. The Metropolitan Board of Works Engineer, Joseph William Bazalgette, devised a plan to build two large sewers, running north and south of the Thames, that would transfer waste to outfalls downstream where it would be released into the outgoing tide. The Southern outfall would run to Crossness and its northern counterpart to point near Barking Creek. In 1860 a contract worth £620,000 was awarded to George Furness to build the northern outfall and its terminal facilities where it met the Thames. In those days the area was an uninhabited wilderness far from the city and did not take the name of Beckton until coming of the Gas Works a decade later.

Initially, a wharf was built at the outfall site for the reception of materials delivered by sea. The sewer itself was built as twin brick tunnels covered in earth and, during its construction from 1861, a standard gauge railway was laid along its course, beginning at the wharf and extending along the route of the works as they progressed. In May that year, one locomotive was working the line but a second engine was engaged by the following month. It is thought the two locos might have come from maker George England's works at New Cross. They were later joined by a Manning Wardle engine (No 44 of 1862 vintage). The site had sidings to gravel pits and a plant to mix concrete, which was then conveyed along the tramway. The contract was completed in 1865, by which time at least five locomotives had been employed, but several are unidentified.

- GE tank loco - details unknown
- GE tank loco - details unknown
- MW 0-6-0ST No 44/1862 *Northern Outfall*

John Mowlem & Company – Northern Outfall Sewage Treatment Works 1887–1889

By 1887 the amount of raw sewage being deposited into the Thames had grown considerably, causing a build up of waste in the river. It was then decided to build a treatment works at the seaward end of the outfall that would provide settlement tanks from which the solids would be loaded into tankers and dumped further out in the estuary. The firm of John Mowlem successfully tendered for the works, which included a new pier, tramway and 12 cottages for a total of £406,000.

The adjacent Gas Light & Coke Company's works had been in operation since 1870 with rail connections to the main line at Custom House, and Mowlem's site at the Sewage Works was served by a standard gauge line connected to the Gas Works railway. The siding was worked by two new locomotives purchased by Mowlem, these being Manning Wardle No 1014 and Hunslet No 338, which stayed until construction was completed in 1889. Afterwards, the siding was purchased by London County Council in 1890 and remained in further use while improvements were carried out to the jetty until 1891.

- MW 0-4-0ST No 1014/1887
- HE 0-4-0ST No 388/1887

An internal tramway of 3ft 6in gauge was also laid around the Sewage Works from 1887 and, over the following years, five locomotives worked its narrow gauge lines (see Chapter 9 "Beckton Sewage Works").

London County Council – Northern Outfall Sewer Widening 1901–1906

Apart from the initial contract carried out by Furness, and afterwards that by Mowlem, there had been several improvement works carried out to both the Sewage Works and the outfall. London County Council was engaged in widening the outfall from 1901 until 1906 and, in the process, used three standard gauge and three narrow gauge engines.

Of the standard engines, MW No 1318 named *Belvedere,* had been transferred from the southern outfall at Crossness in 1902, while another of the same make, MW No 1279 *Talbot*, came via dealers J Wardell & Co the following year. They were joined by Barclay No 992 *Stratford*, which was supplied new in 1904. Of the three smaller engines that were 3ft 6in gauge, Barclay & Co No 272 named *Lea* arrived from T W Ward, Sheffield in 1901, while MW No 1552 *Thames* was supplied new in 1902. Finally, a loco from the lesser known maker of Chapman and Furneaux of Gateshead, No 1151 *Barking*, appeared in the same year.

After the works were completed, *Belvedere* went back to Crossness, *Talbot* was transferred to another London sewage works construction, and *Stratford* was sold to Charles Wall Ltd. *Thames* was sold to B Whitaker & Sons and *Barking* went to William Murphy's contract on the Gold Coast Railway in Africa.

- MW 0-4-0ST No 1318/1896 *Belvedere* (Running No 35)
- MW 0-4-0ST No 1279/1895 *Talbot* (No 36)
- AB 0-4-0ST No 992/1904 *Stratford*

Gauge 3ft 6in locos:

- B 0-4-0ST No 272/1880 *Lea* (No 47)
- MW 0-4-0ST No 1552/1902 *Thames* (No 48)
- CF 0-4-2WT No 1151/1897 *Barking* (No 91)

MW No 1318 "Belvedere" came to Beckton from the Southern Outfall at Crossness and then returned after the works were completed. (Frank Jones Collection/Industrial Locomotive Society)

Peter Lind & Company – Improvements to Northern Out Fall Sewage Works 1931

More work on the outfall took place in 1931 when Peter Lind & Co were employed using a 2ft 0in gauge Hibberd loco No 1731, which was new that year. After Beckton it was transferred to other Lind contracts and afterwards sold to new owners.

- FH 4wPM No 1731/1931 (No 214)

Richard Costain & Sons – Upgrading Northern Outfall Sewer 1935–1938

The outfall was again upgraded in 1935 when Richard Costain was engaged to build new sewage tanks at Beckton. A pair of 2ft 0in gauge Motor Rail locos, Nos 5877 and 5878 were purchased new for the duration of the works which were completed in 1938, when both were transferred to other owners.

Crowley, Russell & Company – New settling tanks and pump foundations 1938–1952

A further 2ft 0in Motor Rail loco, No 7305, appeared later that year when Crowley, Russell & Co were contracted to build new settling tanks and to provide the foundations for new electric pumps. The work was interrupted by the Second World War and finally completed in 1952.

Gauge 2ft 0in

- MR 4wDM No 7305/1938

Edmund Nuttall Sons & Company – New sedimentation tanks for Beckton Sewage Works 1950–1954

In 1950, the sewage works needed new sedimentation tanks and the firm of Edmund Nuttall carried out the works, along with the construction of a nearby outfall sewer at Jenkins Lane, Barking. Five 2ft 0in gauge Ruston locos were engaged in the joint works. Nos 187113, 189948 and 187111 had arrived from the com-

London County Council's 3ft 6in gauge Barclay No 272 "Lea" worked at Beckton but is pictured here elsewhere on its travels. (Russell Wear Collection/Industrial Locomotive Society)

pany's Colnbrook depot by 1951, followed by Nos 200780 and 200781 in 1952.

Of these it is thought only No 200781 remained on the Sewage Works site until completion in 1954. The first pair Nos 187113 and 189948 were sold to the Standard Brick and Sand Company at Redhill, Surrey and No 200780 went to Sykes & Son at Poole, while No 187111 was sold to Pauling & Co at Park Royal in 1952.

Gauge 2ft 0in

- RH 4wDH No 187113/1937 (EN 62)
- RH 4wDH No 189948/1938 (EN 39)
- RH 4wDH No 187111/1937 (EN 68)
- RH 4wDH No 200780/1941 (EN 45)
- RH 4wDH No 200781/1941 (EN 46)

The Demolition & Construction Company – New pier at Beckton Sewage Works 1956 –1957

The Demolition & Construction Company were next on the scene in 1956 with three 2ft 0in gauge locos involved in the building of a new pier for the Sewage Works. Two were Hunslet diesel mechanical types, Nos 4345 and 4300 which came from Higgs & Hill Ltd, and a Ruston, No 217963, that was taken on hire from T W Ward at Hayes. When the works were completed in 1957 the two Hunslets were transferred to Folkestone, where the sea wall was being repaired, and the Ruston went back to Ward's depot.

Gauge 2ft 0in

- HE 4wDM No 4345/1952 (L62)
- HE 4wDM No 4300/1950 (L61)
- RH 4wDM No 217963/1942 (TW2861)

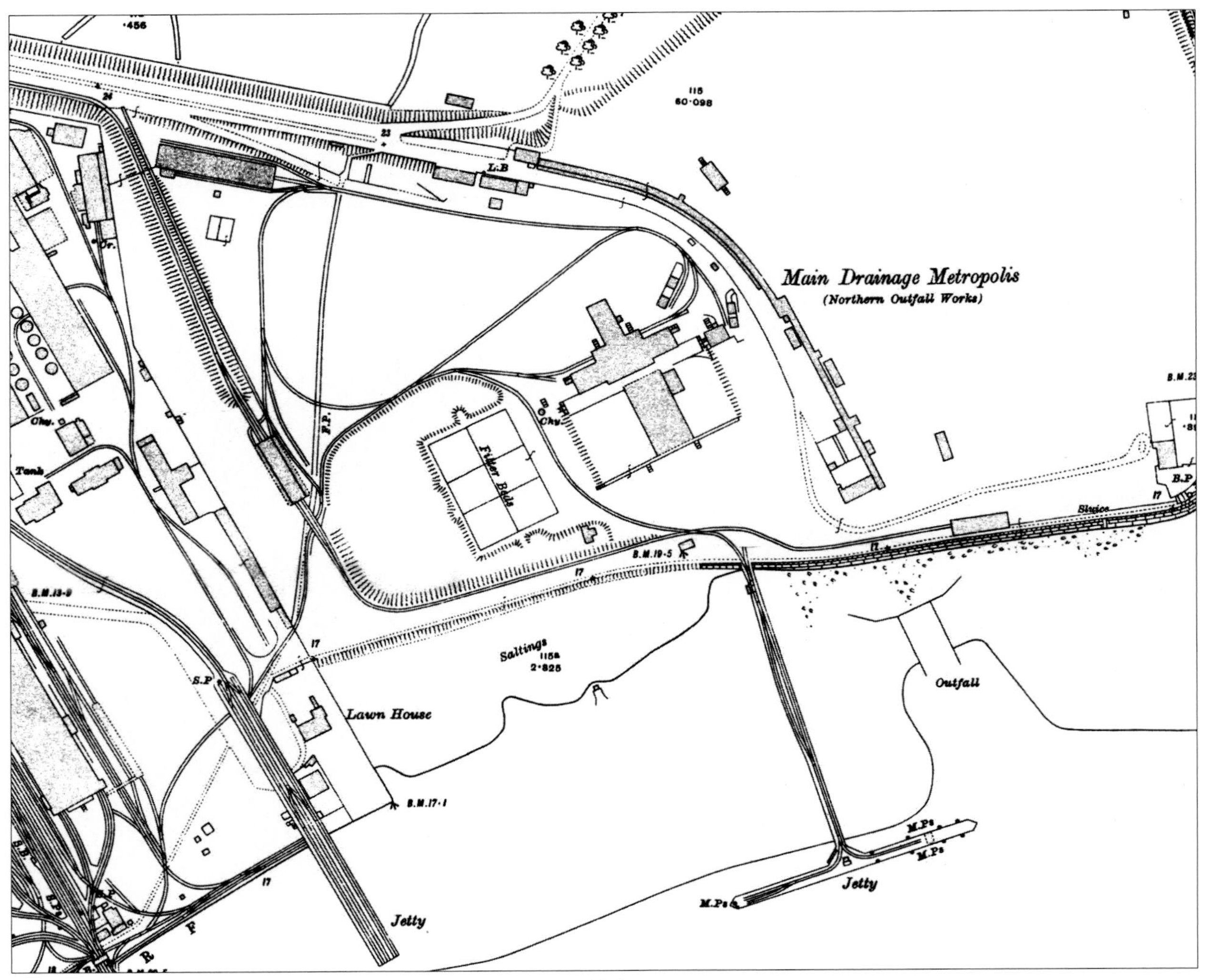

CHAPTER 9

London County Council Beckton Sewage Works 1887-1964

The London County Council Sewage Works at Beckton was built by contractor John Mowlem (see Chapter 8) and its internal 3ft 6in gauge railway served several facilities around the site, including a jetty, an iron water station and a coal store. It also extended along the course of the outfall to a liming station. A standard gauge siding, formerly used by Mowlem, ran to the coal store from a wharf inside the adjacent Gas Works. The siding was purchased by the LCC in February 1890 and remained in use through an agreement with the Gas Light & Coke Company who served the line.

The narrow gauge railway was first operated in 1887 by a new locomotive and wagons supplied by Dick, Kerr & Co and, in 1894, a second loco was purchased new, this being Bagnall No 1424 which was an inverted saddle tank engine. The Dick, Kerr loco was disposed of in 1914 after an Avonside tank engine, No 1668, arrived new in the previous year. No further additions were made until a Baguley four-wheeled petrol loco, No 2081, was acquired new in 1934 but, after the arrival of Ruston No 235743 in 1945, the Baguley was scrapped. By the mid 1940s the section of track along the outfall had been discarded with only rusted remnants of the rails remaining hidden by grass and weeds.

The Bagnall and Ruston locos continued working until the former was scrapped in 1957 and the latter was sold after the railway was abandoned in 1964.

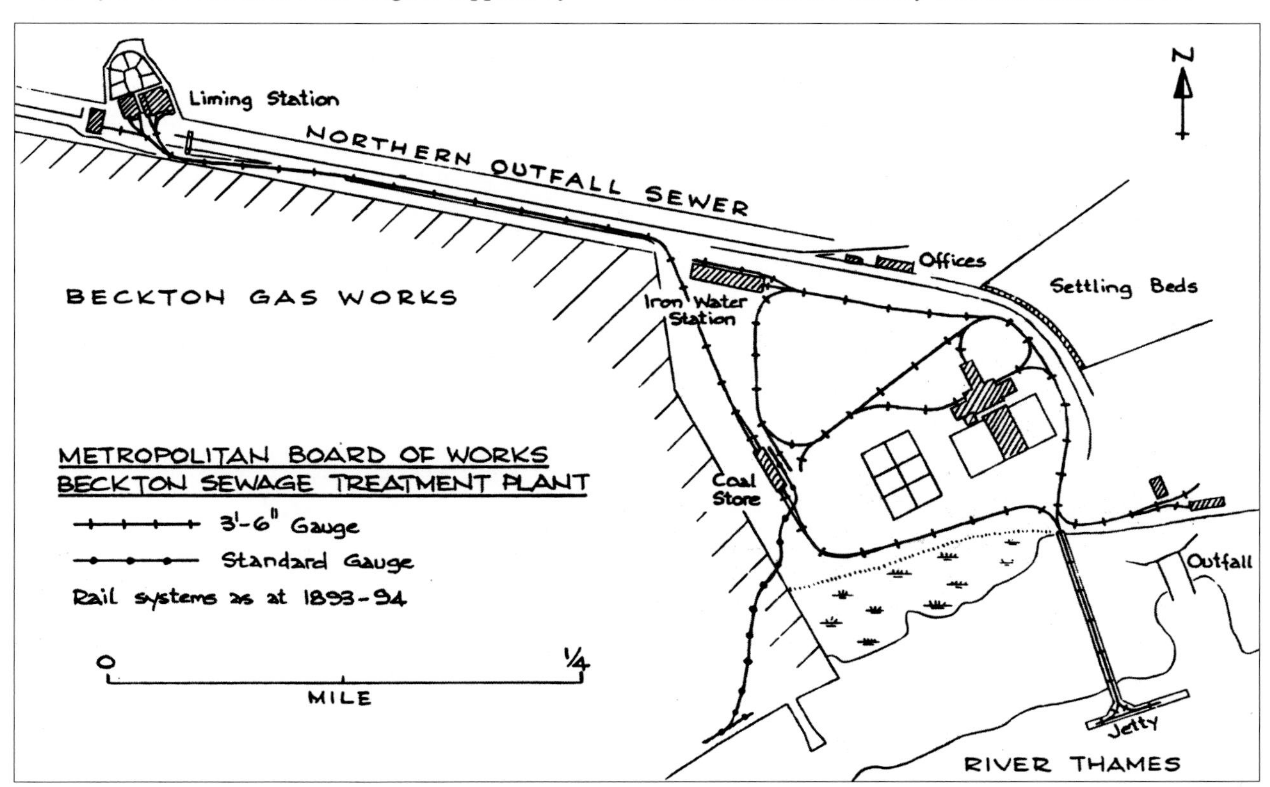

Above: *A diagram of the Beckton Sewage Works narrow gauge railway showing the principal buildings around the site and the standard gauge siding to the coal store running from the adjacent Gas Works. (Industrial Locomotive Society)*

Opposite page: *The narrow gauge railway lines around the Northern Outfall at Beckton in 1914 with the tramway along the outfall course leading off at the top left to the liming station. Part of the gas works system can be seen in the bottom left corner. The sewage works was upgraded many times over the years with several visits by contractors locomotives. (Crown Copyright)*

LCC Beckton Sewage Works 0-4-0ST Dick, Kerr Number not known

Manufacturer:	Dick, Kerr & Co Ltd
Built:	1887
Gauge:	3ft 6in
At Beckton Sewage Works:	1887 – 1914

Very little is known about the Sewage Works first locomotive other than it was built by the firm of Dick, Kerr & Company and arrived at Beckton when the works railway was first laid down in 1887. After being joined by Bagnall No 1424 in 1894, the pair worked together until the DK engine was found to be in poor condition. Despite repairs having been carried out in 1911 and 1912 it was deemed no longer capable of work and replaced by a new Avonside loco (No 1668) in 1913, being finally disposed of for scrap early in 1914.

LCC Beckton Sewage Works 0-4-0IST Bagnall No 1424

Manufacturer:	W G Bagnall Ltd
Built:	1894
Works number:	1424
Running number:	No 2 (18)
Cylinders:	7in x 12in
Driving Wheels:	2ft 0in
Gauge:	3ft 6in
At Beckton Sewage Works:	1894 – 1957

The second loco to work the narrow gauge system at Beckton Sewage Works was Bagnall No 1424, which was an inverted saddle tank engine – that is, the tank was positioned underneath the smokebox and boiler, rather than on top of it. For an unknown reason, it also carried the number 18 on its smokebox door and this number had also been painted on its boiler at some time. Having been dispatched new from the makers on 9th December 1893, it arrived the following month and gave sterling service before being replaced by a Ruston & Hornsby Diesel Mechanical loco No 235743 in 1945, after which it stood out in the open as a spare engine before being scrapped in June 1957 after 64 years service.

LCC Beckton Sewage Works 0-4-0T Avonside No 1668

Manufacturer:	Avonside Engine Company Ltd
Built:	1913
Works number:	1668
Cylinders:	8.5in x 12in
Driving Wheels:	1ft 8in
Gauge:	3ft 6in
At Beckton Sewage Works:	1913 – 1925

The works third locomotive arrived new in 1913 as a replacement for the Dick, Kerr loco which was in poor condition by then. Having served a relatively short period at Beckton it was last reported on site in June 1925 and possibly disposed of around that time.

Old and new at Beckton sewage works with Bagnall No 1424 and a glimpse of its successor, Ruston No 235743 photographed on 5th July 1947. (Jim Peden Collection/Industrial Railway Society)

The second loco at Beckton Sewage Works was Bagnall No 1424, pictured there in May 1949. (Frank Jones/ Author's Collection)

Avonside No 1668 was the sewage works third loco and is pictured at Beckton in 1934. (Frank Jones Collection/ Industrial Locomotive Society)

LCC Beckton Sewage Works 4wPM Baguley No 2081

Manufacturer: EE Baguley Ltd

Built: 1934

Works number: 2081

Engine: 25hp Ford A 3T10C

Gauge: 3ft 6in

At Beckton Sewage Works: 1934 – 1946

This petrol driven loco was despatched new from the makers to Beckton on 25th January 1934. It seems to have led a fairly anonymous existence before being disposed of for scrap in 1946, following the arrival of Ruston No 235743.

LCC Beckton Sewage Works 4wDM Ruston No 235743

Manufacturer: Ruston & Hornsby Ltd

Built: 1945

Works number: 235743

Running number: No 3

Engine: Ruston 4VRO

Weight: 5ton 10cwt

Gauge: 3ft 6in

At Beckton Sewage Works: 1945 – 1965

The final loco to operate the sewage works railway was a Ruston type 48DL No 235743, which left the makers for Beckton on 7th August 1945, immediately replacing the Baguley engine and demoting its Bagnall partner to the status of spare engine. After the line was abandoned in early 1964, the Ruston was sold to shipbreakers Ronald L Baker at Pitsea Wharf, Essex around August 1965 where it was stored in a derelict state until scrapped some time after May 1972.

Summary of locomotives at Beckton Sewage Works						
Maker	**Works No**	**Date Built**	**Type**	**Running No**	**Date Arrived**	**Date Departed**
DK	?	1887	0-4-0ST	n/a	1887	1914
WB	1424	1894	0-4-0IST	No 2	1894	1957
AE	1668	1913	0-4-0T	n/a	1913	1925
Bg/DC	2081	1934	4wPM	n/a	1934	1946
RH	235743	1945	4wDM	No 3	1945	1965

Index